The
Rottweiler

An Owner's Guide To

A HAPPY HEALTHY PET

Howell Book House

Howell Book House
A Simon & Schuster Macmillan Company
1633 Broadway
New York, NY 10019

MACMILLAN is a registered trademark of Macmillan, Inc.

Library of Congress Cataloging-in-Publication Data
Forster, Jean.
    The Rottweiler: an owner's guide to a happy, healthy pet/by Jean Forster.
    p.cm.
    Includes bibliographical references.
    ISBN 0–87605–379–7
    1. Rottweiler dog. I. Title.
SF429.R7F67 1995
636.7'3—dc20   95–24282
    CIP

Manufactured in the United States of America
10 9 8 7 6

Series Director: Dominique De Vito
Series Assistant Director: Felice Primeau
Book Design: Michele Laseau
Cover Design: Iris Jeromnimon
Illustration: Jeff Yesh
Photography:
  Cover by Kerrin Winter & Dale Churchill; puppy by Pets by Paulette
  Joan Balzarini: 96
  Mary Bloom: 42, 96, 136, 145
  Paulette Braun/Pets by Paulette: 2–3, 5, 7, 8, 9, 12, 34–35, 39, 44, 96
  Buckinghamhill American Cocker Spaniels: 148
  Sian Cox: 134
  Dr. Ian Dunbar: 98, 101, 103, 111, 116–117, 122, 123, 127
  Jean Forster: 25, 29
  Shari Kathol: 27, 46, 47, 48, 58, 60, 62, 67, 94
  Dan Lyons: 96
  Cathy Merrithew: 129
  Liz Palika: 133
  Janice Raines: 132
  Susan Rezy: 96–97
  Judith Strom: 11, 17, 19, 21, 23, 26, 30, 36, 45, 52, 57, 63, 81, 96, 107, 110, 128, 130,
    135, 137, 139, 140, 144, 149, 150
Production Team: Troy Barnes, John Carroll, Jama Carter,
  Kathleen Caulfield, Trudy Coler, Vic Peterson, Terri Sheehan,
  Marvin Van Tiem, Amy DeAngelis and Kathy Iwasaki

Contents

Welcome

to the

World

of the

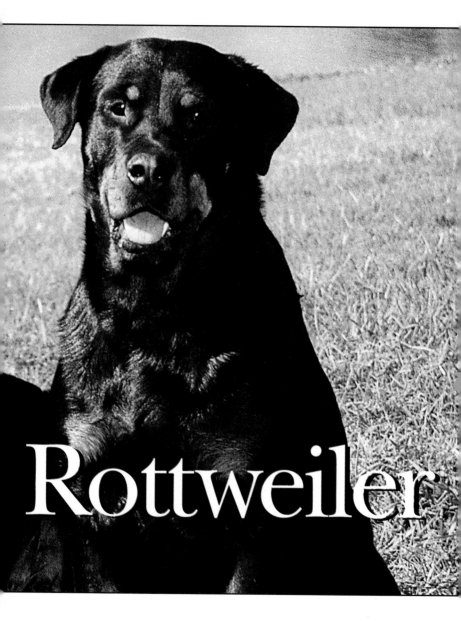

part one

Rottweiler

External Features of the Rottweiler

chapter 1

What
is a
Rottweiler?

Any definition of the Rottweiler would be incomplete without an explanation of the official standard of the breed. Each standard is prepared by the national breed club and approved by the American Kennel Club (AKC), the principal registry of purebred dogs in the United States. The standard provides a physical description of the breed with limited reference to temperament. The disqualifications noted in a standard are those things that prohibit the dog from competing with others of its breed for the required number of points necessary to be designated as a breed champion by the AKC. The serious faults noted prevent a dog from competing successfully. Reading a standard is dry and boring work; however, if you want a Rottweiler that really looks like a Rottweiler, you should familiarize yourself with what is and is not desirable.

Official Standard for the Rottweiler (Effective June 28, 1990)

General Appearance—The ideal Rottweiler is a medium large, robust and powerful dog, black with clearly defined rust markings. His compact and substantial build denotes great strength, agility and endurance. Dogs are characteristically more massive throughout with larger frame and heavier bone than bitches. Bitches are distinctly feminine but without weakness of substance or structure.

Size, Proportion, Substance Dogs—24 inches to 27 inches. Bitches—22 inches to 25 inches, with preferred size being mid-range of each sex. Correct proportion is of primary importance, as long as size is within the standard's range. The length of body, from prosternum to the rearmost projection of the rump, is slightly longer than the height of the dog at the withers, the most desirable proportion of the height to length being 9 to 10. The Rottweiler is neither coarse nor shelly. Depth of chest is approximately fifty percent (50%) of the height of the dog. His bone and muscle mass must be sufficient to balance his frame, giving a compact and very powerful appearance. Serious Faults—Lack of proportion, undersized, oversized, reversal of sex characteristics (bitchy dogs, doggy bitches).

WHAT IS A BREED STANDARD?

A breed standard—a detailed description of an individual breed—is meant to portray the *ideal* specimen of that breed. This includes ideal structure, temperament, gait, type—all aspects of the dog. Because the standard describes an ideal specimen, it isn't based on any particular dog. It is a concept against which judges compare actual dogs and breeders strive to produce dogs. At a dog show, the dog that wins is the one that comes closest, in the judge's opinion, to the standard for its breed. Breed standards are written by the breed parent clubs, the national organizations formed to oversee the well-being of the breed. They are voted on and approved by the members of the parent clubs.

Head—Of medium length, broad between the ears; forehead line seen in profile is moderately arched; zygomatic arch and stop well developed with strong broad upper and lower jaws. The desired ratio of backskull to muzzle is 3 to 2. Forehead is preferred dry, however some wrinkling may occur when dog is alert. *Expression* is noble, alert, and self-assured. *Eyes* of medium size, almond shaped with well fitting lids, moderately deep-set, neither protruding nor receding. The desired color is a uniform dark brown. Serious Faults— Yellow (bird of prey) eyes, eyes of different color or size, hairless eye rim. Disqualifications—Entropion, Ectropion. *Ears* of medium size, pendant, triangular in shape; when carried alertly the ears are level with the top of the skull and appear to broaden it. Ears are to be set well apart, hanging forward with the inner edge lying tightly against the head and terminating at approximately mid-cheek. Serious Faults— Improper carriage (creased, folded or held away from cheek/head). *Muzzle*—Bridge is straight, broad at base with slight tapering towards tip. The end of the muzzle is broad with well developed chin. *Nose* is broad rather than round and always black. *Lips*—Always black; corners closed; inner mouth pigment is preferred dark. Serious Faults—Total lack of mouth pigment (pink mouth). *Bite and Dentition*—Teeth 42 in number (20 upper, 22 lower), strong, correctly placed, meeting in a scissors bite—lower incisors touching inside of upper incisors. Serious Faults—Level bite; any missing tooth. Disqualifications—Overshot, undershot (when incisors do not touch or mesh); wry mouth; two or more missing teeth.

Neck, Topline, Body. *Neck*—Powerful, well muscled, moderately long, slightly arched and without loose skin. *Topline*— The back is firm and level, extending in a straight line from behind the withers to the croup. The back remains horizontal to the ground while the dog is moving or standing. *Body*—The chest is roomy, broad and deep, reaching to elbow, with well pronounced forechest and well sprung, oval ribs. Back is straight and strong. Loin is short, deep and well muscled.

The Rottweiler is a robust and powerful dog.

Croup is broad, of medium length and only slightly sloping. Underline of a mature Rottweiler has a slight tuck-up. Males must have two normal testicles properly descended into the scrotum. Disqualifications—Unilateral cryptorchid or

The Rottweiler's expression is noble and alert.

cryptorchid males. *Tail*—Tail docked short, close to body, leaving one or two tail vertebrae. The set of the tail is more important than length. Properly set, it gives an impression of elongation of topline; carried slightly above horizontal when the dog is excited or moving.

Forequarters—Shoulder blade is long and well laid back. Upper arm equal in length to shoulder blade, set so elbows are well under body. Distance from withers to elbow and elbow to ground is equal. Legs are strongly developed with straight, heavy bone, not set close together. Pasterns are strong, springy and almost perpendicular to the ground. Feet are round, compact with well arched toes, turning neither in nor out. Pads are thick and hard. Nails short, strong and black. Dewclaws may be removed.

Hindquarters—Angulation of hindquarters balances that of forequarters. Upper thigh is fairly long, very broad and well muscled. Stifle joint is well turned. Lower thigh is long, broad and powerful, with extensive muscling leading into a strong hock joint. Rear pasterns are nearly perpendicular to the ground. Viewed from the rear, hind legs are straight, strong and wide enough apart to fit with a properly built body. Feet are somewhat longer than the front feet, turning neither in nor out, equally compact with well arched toes. Pads are thick and hard. Nails short, strong, and black. Dewclaws must be removed.

Coat—Outer coat is straight, coarse, dense, of medium length and lying flat. Undercoat should be present on neck and thighs, but the amount is influenced by climatic conditions. Undercoat should not show through outer coat. The coat is shortest on head, ears and legs, longest on breeching. The Rottweiler is to be exhibited in the natural condition with no trimming. Fault—Wavy coat. Serious Faults—Open, excessively short, or curly coat; total lack of undercoat; any trimming that alters the length of the natural coat. Disqualifications—Long coat.

8

Color—Always black with rust to mahogany markings. The demarcation between black and rust is to be clearly defined. The markings should be located as follows: a spot over each eye; on cheeks; as a strip around each side of muzzle, but not on the bridge of nose; on throat; triangular mark on both sides of prosternum; on forelegs from carpus downward to the toes; on inside of rear legs showing down the front of the stifle and broadening out to front of rear legs from hock to toes but not completely eliminating black from rear of pasterns; under tail; black penciling on toes. The undercoat is gray, tan, or black. Quantity and location of rust markings is important and should not exceed ten percent of body color. Serious Faults—Straw colored, excessive, insufficient or sooty markings; rust marking other than described above; white marking any place on dog (a few rust or white hairs do not constitute a marking). Disqualifications—Any base color other than black; absence of all markings.

Gait—The Rottweiler is a trotter. His movement should be balanced, harmonious, sure, powerful and unhindered, with strong forereach and a powerful rear drive. The motion is effortless, efficient, and ground covering. Front and rear legs are thrown neither in nor out, as the imprint of hind feet should touch that of forefeet. In a trot the forequarters and hindquarters are mutually coordinated while the back remains level, firm and relatively motionless. As speed increases the legs will converge under body towards a center line.

Rottweilers are self-confident and adaptable.

Temperament—The Rottweiler is basically a calm, confident and courageous dog with a self-assured aloofness that does not lend itself to immediate and indiscriminate friendships. A Rottweiler is self-confident and responds quietly and with a wait-and-see attitude to influences in his environment. He has an inherent desire to protect home and family, and is an intelligent dog of extreme hardness and adaptability with a strong willingness to work, making him especially suited as a companion, guardian and general all-purpose dog. The behavior of the

Rottweiler in the show ring should be controlled, willing and adaptable, trained to submit to examination of mouth, testicles, etc. An aloof or reserved dog should not be penalized as this reflects the accepted character of the breed. An aggressive or belligerent attitude towards other dogs should not be faulted. A judge shall excuse from the ring any shy Rottweiler. A dog shall be judged fundamentally shy if, refusing to stand for examination, it shrinks away from the judge. A dog that in the opinion of the judge menaces or threatens him/her, or exhibits any sign that it may not be safely approached or examined by the judge in the normal manner, shall be excused from the ring. A dog that in the opinion of the judge attacks any person in the ring shall be disqualified.

Summary—The foregoing is a description of the ideal Rottweiler. Any structural fault that detracts from the above described working dog must be penalized to the extent of the deviation.

Disqualifications—Entropion, ectropion. Overshot, undershot (when incisors do not touch or mesh); wry mouth: two or more missing teeth. Unilateral cryptorchid or cryptorchid males. Long coat. Any base color other than black; absence of all markings. A dog that in the opinion of the judge attacks any person in the ring.

THE AMERICAN KENNEL CLUB

Familiarly referred to as "the AKC," the American Kennel Club is a nonprofit organization devoted to the advancement of purebred dogs. The AKC maintains a registry of recognized breeds and adopts and enforces rules for dog events including shows, obedience trials, field trials, hunting tests, lure coursing, herding, earthdog trials, agility and the Canine Good Citizen program. It is a club of clubs, established in 1884 and composed, today, of over 500 autonomous dog clubs throughout the United States. Each club is represented by a delegate; the delegates make up the legislative body of the AKC, voting on rules and electing directors. The American Kennel Club maintains the Stud Book, the record of every dog ever registered with the AKC, and publishes a variety of materials on purebred dogs, including a monthly magazine, books and numerous educational pamphlets. For more information, contact the AKC at the address listed in Chapter 13, "Resources," and look for the names of their publications in Chapter 12, "Recommended Reading."

Another Look at the Standard

How important is the standard to you in selecting your Rottweiler? It can be of great value if you understand that the standard represents an ideal but that few things in life come close to being ideal. In choosing a Rottweiler, you have obviously some idea of how the dog looks. Let's do some fine-tuning and see how the standard can aid you in determining what might be a suitable animal for you.

Size, Proportion, Substance—Obviously, the standard does not describe a giant breed such as a Great Dane or Saint Bernard. Neither does it describe a dog the size of a Spaniel. First and foremost, the Rottweiler is a working dog. If too large, the dog is usually too clumsy and awkward; if too small, the dog lacks the strength and power to do the work it was bred for.

Advertisements are frequently seen for puppies from parents weighing 160 to 180 pounds. These Rottweilers are either grossly overweight, or their size is grossly exaggerated.

Head: Eyes—Yellow eyes will not affect a dog's ability to be a good companion, although the color certainly does alter its facial expression. However, eyes of different size or color make one wonder what other genetic flaws may be present. Hairless eye rim can be a serious health problem. The skin may grow coarse, puffy or itchy, causing the dog to paw at it or rub it against furniture or carpet. This may abrade the skin or injure the eye. Entropion (where the eyelid turns inward) and ectropion (where the eyelid rolls away from the eye) are serious flaws. Both can only be corrected surgically. If surgery is performed at an early age, it may again be necessary when the dog matures. Avoid puppies that display this characteristic or whose parents display it.

Remember, the Rottweiler is built to work.

Muzzle—Certainly a pink mouth will not interfere with a dog's ability to be a great companion. This condition is thought to be inherited and happens in the finest of breedings.

Bite and Dentition—A Rottweiler with a level bite or one that is overshot or undershot is still an excellent candidate for the pet owner. However, dogs with wry mouth (where jaws do not align) or grossly overshot or undershot bites may have serious problems with eating. Form follows function.

Rottweilers that seriously deviate from the descriptions listed in "Body," "Forequarters," and "Hindquarters" may be seriously handicapped in their mobility. Coat— There is no room for personal preference. Rottweilers are black with rust to mahogany markings. Period. This breed has not had any other breed crossed into its bloodlines for one hundred years. There is no genetic reason for Rottweilers to have a base coat other than black. Total absence of markings may indicate questionable ancestry. White, gold and red Rottweilers have been advertised, but the reader should be warned that these dogs may not be shown, should not be bred and are seriously challenged when AKC registration is attempted. If you want a Rottweiler, you want a black dog with rust to mahogany markings.

No matter how handsome, it's temperament you live with 365 days a year.

Temperament—It cannot be said often enough that the Rottweiler was bred to work. Not only is the dog extremely quick to learn the things its owner teaches, but also it has a remarkable ability to figure out things without benefit of instruction. This dog, for many years, went about its job as drover, guardian, police dog or military dog with a minimum of fuss. In October 1984, the AKC registered 440 Rottweiler litters and 1,751 individual Rottweilers; in September 1994, the AKC registered 2,285 Rottweiler litters and 7,689 individual Rottweilers. In those ten years, the gene pool expanded so greatly and so randomly as to seriously influence the marvelous temperament of this breed. We now see Rottweilers ranging from shy, timid and hysterical to mindlessly aggressive (dogs that are too hard even for police or military work).

There are many physical flaws that a pet owner can choose to rise above, provided the dog is not in discomfort and the effect on your wallet is not too great. No one can or should choose to ignore bad temperament. Shy dogs are as dangerous as aggressive dogs because they frequently bite in fear when cornered or threatened even if no mischief is intended by the person involved. Temperament is what you live with 365 days a year; it's what makes a dog a joy to have around or a pressure cooker waiting to explode.

chapter 2

The Rottweiler's Ancestry

History tells us that when the Romans invaded Europe, they did so with vast armies, which required vast supplies of food. Much of this food was beef on the hoof, so the journey required using many dogs to act as drovers and guard dogs for the herds. These dogs were of no particular breed, but in general resembled the Mastiff; they were large and powerful, courageous and steadfast—a formidable force. They endured the freezing cold of the mountains and the heat of the valleys. If an accident, injury or poor health overcame them, like the soldiers they accompanied, they either died or got better.

Many Romans settled on the banks of the Neckar River, whose climate and soil combined to provide an ideal place for raising cattle. It can only be assumed that during the next few hundred years, descendants of the dogs that crossed the Alps with the Romans continued their role as guardian and drover's dog. The settlement flourished and became a major trade and cattle center. Butchers were an important part of the community, and their dogs were known as *Metzgerhunds* (butcher dogs).

Red Tile Town Dogs

Because of the red-tiled roofing on some of the original Roman buildings, the town became known as Rote Wil (Red Tile). Eventually it was called Rottweil, and the working cattle dogs from there were called Rottweilers. Other than the nobility or aristocracy, people in those days would not or could not afford to feed any animal that did not earn its keep. The larger dogs were used by the butchers to drive cattle as well as to guard them in the pens before butchering. It is said that smaller specimens of this breed that had derived from the Roman dogs were used for more domestic work at the butcher's home. The dogs would walk treadmills to turn spits and herd geese and ducks.

One would imagine that, especially as puppies, the dogs doubled as playmates for the children. The story is told (and many paintings have been made of the subject) that on Saturday—a busy trading day—the butcher would be inclined to stop at the local tavern before wending his way home. Fearful that too much imbibing would render him incapable of protecting the money he had earned that day, he would place the coins in a leather pouch and tie the pouch around the neck of his Rottweiler. Fact or fiction, today many Rottweiler owners protect small valuables in the same fashion.

Finding a New Job

About the middle of the nineteenth century, a law was passed forbidding the driving of cattle over roads; almost simultaneously, the railroad and the donkey replaced the Rottweiler as a cart dog. A few years before World War I, only one Rottweiler bitch existed in the town of Rottweil. In 1901, efforts were made to

FAMOUS OWNERS OF ROTTWEILERS

Shannon Doherty

John Larroquette

Barry Larkin

Jack Scalia

Christian Slater

Randy White

Stevie Wonder

form a Rottweiler (and Leonberger) Club. The club did not last long but can take credit for producing the first Rottweiler standard. Longtime Rottweiler breeders tell us there have been no notable changes in the physical requirements for the breed and no changes at all from the character and temperament originally specified.

The work ethic was implanted in the Rottweiler during its development in Germany. The farmers and butchers cared little for aesthetic appearance in a dog; if a good working bitch came in season and a good working male was available, a breeding sometimes took place. If the bitch conceived and whelped, any malformed, unthrifty and weak puppies were destroyed. Additional culling took place at a later time— if the dog didn't work it didn't survive. "A good working dog is eager to work and is the worse for not being used." In the Rottweiler, "a definite change has been seen if the dog is never taught or permitted to work. He may become surly, he may no longer seek or permit affection, he may become lethargic and indifferent to his surroundings." The foregoing quotes are from an article I wrote for *Dog Sports* magazine in February 1979. It was true then, and it is true now.

In my opinion, the Rottweiler, precisely because of his need for work, should not grow up in a kennel, because his instinct is not satisfied there. The more the Rottweiler is kept busy, the better his abilities will develop, for his whole being strives for work and action.

WHERE DID DOGS COME FROM?

It can be argued that dogs were right there at man's side from the beginning of time. As soon as human beings began to document their existence, the dog was among their drawings and inscriptions. Dogs were not just friends, they served a purpose: There were dogs to hunt birds, pull sleds, herd sheep, burrow after rats—even sit in laps! What your dog was originally bred to do influences the way it behaves. The American Kennel Club recognizes over 140 breeds, and there are hundreds more distinct breeds around the world. To make sense of the breeds, they are grouped according to their size or function. The AKC has seven groups:

1) Sporting, 2) Working,
3) Herding, 4) Hounds,
5) Terriers, 6) Toys,
7) Nonsporting

Can you name a breed from each group? Here's some help: (1) Golden Retriever; (2) Doberman Pinscher; (3) Collie; (4) Beagle; (5) Scottish Terrier; (6) Maltese; and (7) Dalmatian. All modern domestic dogs (*Canis familiaris*) are related, however different they look, and are all descended from *Canis lupus*, the gray wolf.

The Rottweiler in the U.S.

Rottweilers were imported into this country by their German owners who emigrated here and by Americans who had visited Germany and had been impressed by the Rottweiler. In 1931, the first Rottweiler was listed in the AKC Stud Book, and for a time the breed enjoyed a slow increase in popularity. After World War II, however, returning servicemen who had been stationed in Germany and seen this breed do its work in the military, railroad yards and so forth were quick to try to import animals for their own use. They were not so much interested in show or breeding stock but wanted dogs that would *work*! Many of these men naturally gravitated from the military into law enforcement or private security.

The Rottweiler was—and is— a drover and herder.

Many of the Germans who emigrated after World War II brought with them their love for the sport of *Schutzhund*—quite literally, "safe dog"; Schutzhund is a competition sport with quite rigid rules. Essentially, the dog must pass the required tests for tracking, obedience and protection work—all on the same day. Not only is performance judged, but also temperament. Although the sport of Schutzhund was originally developed as a test for the suitability of a German Shepherd, it was quickly expanded to encompass many of the breeds designated as Working dogs, and the Rottweiler gained an enviable reputation in this sport, one it still enjoys today.

By this time, it had become the in thing to own a pure-bred dog registered with the AKC. It neither mattered whether it was a correct representative of the breed nor what kind of temperament or needs the dog had. The rarer the breed, the higher the status of the owner. Such rarity usually commands a pretty stiff purchase price; buyers decided that breeding the dog and selling the offspring for an equally high price would not only recoup their original investment, but show a tidy profit to boot! Having little or no knowledge of canine genetics and even less insight into proper rearing and training of such a determined animal as the Rottweiler, these owners embarked on a course that could only be detrimental to the breed.

Odo v Gaisburg, a great dog of the past.

The Rise— and Fall— of the Rottweiler

While knowledgeable and ethical breeders pored over pedigrees, looking for the right stud dog for their bitch, while they X-rayed hips and elbows to determine that their breeding stock was free from genetic skeletal problems, while they carefully evaluated temperament in their dogs, Fred and Ethel merrily bred any dog to any bitch, neglecting to do any screening of breeding stock or potential puppy buyers. Coincidentally, the crime rate in America started a sharp upswing, and suddenly people who hadn't the proverbial pot or the window to throw it out of felt that they had to have a "guard dog."

Probably no recognized breed has suffered from "celebrity ownership" as much as the Rottweiler has. Everyone from rock stars to entire football teams have been Rottweiler owners. One player confessed that he was so paranoid he had two Rottweilers guarding him while he slept in a room resembling an arsenal. I had the unsettling experience of being on hand when a country-and-western singer was scheduled to appear at a trainer's kennel to learn how to handle his Rottweiler, which he had sent to the trainer for "protection training." I knew the trainer very well and had considerable respect for his ability and integrity.

The Rottweiler was a nice-looking, nicely behaved dog, and when his owner appeared, the dog was put through his paces. Using a decoy wearing protective padding, the trainer handled the dog through a series of demonstrations; when the decoy attempted to "mug" the trainer, the dog attacked and bit. When the trainer gave the command for the dog to stop, the animal immediately released his hold and returned to the trainer. The dog performed without a hitch and with great enthusiasm. I turned to the singer, intending to compliment him on his dog. The poor man's face was absolutely ashen, and he had broken out in a cold sweat. The trainer gave him verbal instructions on what to say to the dog and suggested that the first time the dog should be on leash, held by his owner. No bite would be allowed the first few times in order that the owner might get a feel for the dog's behavior; conse-

quently, the decoy wore no protective gear. When the decoy appeared and shouted insults at the dog's owner, the dog barked and lunged, and the owner threw the leash in the air, turned and ran! This left the decoy on the field with an angry dog charging him. Fortunately, the trainer was on his toes and stopped the dog with a single command. All the money in the world would not qualify that dog's owner to take charge of the dog.

With proper training, Rottweilers make excellent police dogs.

Not too many years ago a story made the rounds about a noted sportscaster who bought a Rottweiler. After the dog was mature, the announcer and his wife were approached by a man who came to their door, proclaimed himself a trainer of protection dogs and offered to train their Rottweiler. They heartily agreed, having no idea what this meant. Every day the self-ordained trainer would come and open the front door, yelling and shouting, and the dog would run to the door and bite the padded sleeve the man stuck through it. You can almost guess the inevitable result. Eventually, at approximately the same time the dog was used to expecting the invasion of his territory, a neighbor came through the door and was promptly bitten. Such action can best be described as a violation of the Dumb Person's Act, Section 1, of the Stupid Code.

Equally irresponsible acts are reported regularly, some having tragic consequences. The media dutifully report these incidents on the six o'clock news, and talk shows spotlight the Rottweiler as a "killer dog." Such publicity has not gone unnoticed by your neighborhood criminal. People outside the law have purchased Rottweilers for their own nefarious purposes—to guard their marijuana plantations, to guard their stash of cocaine, to guard their illegal weapons and also to participate in that reprehensible activity—pitting dogs against each other in fights to the death.

An 1890 photo of a woman and a Rottweiler pulling a cart.

Loved for the Right Reasons

Fortunately, the majority of Rottweiler owners love, understand and respect the breed. Rottweilers have become widely recognized for their excellent work as therapy dogs; their owners visit hospitals and nursing homes, and the dogs are trained to be gentle "angels of mercy." They are taught not to put their feet on a patient's bed (it may cause pain to the patient), not to lean against anyone (a patient may be too weak to withstand the pressure of a large dog) and to move calmly and quietly.

In many juvenile facilities, especially those which house abused children, it's not uncommon for a child who has been unable to utter a word to an adult to unreservedly share feelings with a dog. Many years ago I took a large, impressive male—a working police canine—to a safe house for juveniles. Our presence had been requested to demonstrate the dog's friendliness. One small girl refused to enter the room where the dogs were doing tricks. My dog was wearing a backpack full of candy, and the children were delighted to have the dog approach them so they could reach into the pack and select a candy bar. But the small girl remained in the doorway of an adjacent room.

When we had finished our program, said good-bye and headed for the exit, the small girl darted out, firmly took my dog by his collar and led him into the other room. I was quite startled because this dog had previously refused to let anyone but me lead him anywhere by any means. I stepped to the door of the room the pair had disappeared into and saw a moving sight. The child had clasped her arms tightly around the dog's neck and was sobbing uncontrollably. The dog was sitting, looking very worried; he placed a huge paw gently on her shoulder, and gradually, the tears subsided. She whispered something in his ear—who knows what—then took hold of his collar again and led him back to me. The dog wore an expression of pleasure mixed with embarrassment; the child was smiling. "Can he come back tomorrow?" she whispered. When the counselor told me these were the first words she had spoken in weeks, I assured her we would be back tomorrow, and back we went every day for the entire week.

Rottweilers are versatile companions.

The Rottweiler continues to enjoy prestige as a versatile dog for law enforcement; in addition, a keen sense of smell and dedication to duty make the dog frequently the breed of choice for many search and rescue groups. The Rottweiler's strong instinct to control livestock has made the breed a popular choice as a ranch dog. Recently, the AKC acknowledged the Rottweiler's ability as a herder by permitting the breed to compete in AKC-sanctioned herding trials, formerly limited to those breeds in the Herding group. Many owners utilize the Rottweiler's strength and endurance by teaching their dogs to pull a cart or sled. Although not breaking any speed records, the breed has tremendous power and seems to enjoy this activity. Many have achieved recognition by competing in weight-pulling contests.

In short, Rottweilers enjoy most activities involving their owners and physical energy because the breed was genetically engineered to be physically, mentally and emotionally active.

chapter 3

The **World**
According to the
Rottweiler

No single phrase describing the Rottweiler's character and temperament can apply to each Rottweiler; there are variations in these qualities as there are variations in size, health, personality and so on; however, properly bred, properly reared Rottweilers share many similarities. For example, most Rottweilers are quite territorial and demonstrate a strong instinct to defend their turf. They may be quite vocal and  aggressive toward strangers invading their space. This territory may sometimes extend beyond reason, usually when a dog has not had guidance in understanding the limits of its responsibilities.

Understanding "Prey Drive"

The dog still retains many primitive drives of his wolf ancestors. One of these is the "prey" drive, the force that motivated the animal to chase and catch its food. Trainers utilize this prey drive to this very day in training hunting dogs and in racing greyhounds. In those breeds selectively bred to emphasize guarding and protection instincts, the prey drive often manifests itself as the desire to chase (and catch) that which runs. It's a small step from chasing running deer (in herds or individually) to chasing running humans, particularly children, who tend to emit the same shrill sounds that prey might utter.

It's your responsibility to make absolutely certain your Rottweiler cannot pursue this activity. Rottweilers maintained behind fences that face busy streets or streets on which there is a lot of foot traffic will quickly learn to threaten passersby. The level of frustration will build until, if the opportunity presents itself, the dog is ready to bite. Most dogs cannot hold eye contact with humans for more than a few seconds. Many Rottweilers prove the exception to this rule. By their actions, some almost demand eye contact. If it's prolonged, the dog may perceive it as a challenge and begin to posture and flex its muscles by growling with increasing menace.

Frequently, males (and sometimes females) are extremely aggressive toward other dogs,

---

A DOG'S SENSES

Sight: With their eyes located farther apart than ours, dogs can detect movement at a greater distance than we can, but they can't see as well up close. They can also see better in less light, but can't distinguish many colors.

Sound: Dogs can hear about four times better than we can, and they can hear high-pitched sounds especially well. Their ancestors, the wolves, howled to let other wolves know where they were; our dogs do the same, but they have a wider range of vocalizations, including barks, whimpers, moans and whines.

Smell: A dog's nose is his greatest sensory organ. His sense of smell is so great he can follow a trail that's weeks old, detect odors diluted to one-millionth the concentration we'd need to notice them, even sniff out a person under water!

Taste: Dogs have fewer taste buds than we do, so they're likelier to try anything—and usually do, which is why it's especially important for their owners to monitor their food intake. Dogs are omnivores, which means they eat meat as well as vegetable matter like grasses and weeds.

Touch: Dogs are social animals and love to be petted, groomed and played with.

particularly of the same sex. Again, this problem usually arises because the dog has not been schooled in what is acceptable behavior. Many of my Rottweilers served as police canines; off duty, in their yard, they could be just as loud and foolish as any other dog challenging a canine trespasser. However, such behavior would not be tolerated on duty. If I had to send a dog into an alley after a bad guy, it would be unacceptable behavior for the dog to have a confrontation with every animal he passed.

To the Rottweiler the world is his.

With proper training the Rottweiler can be taught to ignore casual encounters with other dogs. It's fairly evident how the true Rottweiler perceives the world: *it's his*! Rottweilers can be quite pushy and "bossy"; they can be overly possessive not just of favorite toys, bones and people, but also of really silly things like the water in their buckets. This guarding instinct is wonderful when properly channeled; unpleasant if carried to uncontrollable extremes.

Singing Rottweilers

Many Rottweilers are quite vocal in expressing their feelings; in addition to the barking, growling and whining common to all breeds, many Rottweilers appreciate a good songfest and will throw back their heads and howl with vigor. Some Rottweilers (particularly males) will rumble deep in their chests a sort of purring, to express pleasure at having their tummies scratched or their ears massaged.

For those who cannot distinguish between a threatening growl and a contented purr, this experience can be disturbing. Most Rottweilers seem to enjoy having things in their mouths—sticks, bones, toys, balls—some like to place their mouths gently over their owners' hands and lead them around; some play tug-of-war with their leashes. Although you may find the latter two actions amusing, they are best curbed at an early age because such behavior is a form of subtle dominance of the dog over you. I never met a Rottweiler who didn't love to dig for gophers or ground squirrels; it's not unusual for a Rottweiler to display great interest in objects above its head—birds, airplanes, hot-air balloons and so forth.

A most endearing trait of this breed, perhaps in contrast to its strength and determination, is its almost clownish playfulness. Rottweilers can entertain themselves for hours lying on their back, spinning a ball or other toy between their forepaws. Rottweilers that are really crazy about balls will sometimes have a game of catch all by themselves. Grabbing the ball in their mouths, they will fling it into the air then run to catch it before it hits the ground, for all the world like an outfielder. Tiring of that, they will throw the ball across the yard, bounding after it with great glee. Frequently, they throw their entire body directly on top of the ball then pretend not to know where it is.

It's easy to teach a Rottweiler to retrieve.

Such an attitude makes the Rottweiler an easy pupil to teach the retrieve. Mine have saved me countless steps by fetching objects from another room as well as finding lost objects for me.

Adolescent Rottweilers can be quite rowdy and boisterous; many are prone to be "body slammers." Having some eighty pounds or more impact, their bodies can be detrimental to your health! Rottweilers can be taught to be more circumspect and respectful of your person as they reach maturity; however, their exposure to small children, the very elderly or the physically enfeebled should never be without supervision.

Usually first-time owners are surprised and delighted to have their Rottweiler youngster voluntarily follow them from room to room. This behavior does *not* indicate insecurity in the dog; neither is it proof of slavish devotion. The simple fact is that Rottweilers *like* to have their favorite people in view. When the owner leaves the room, the dog will usually wait a few minutes, anticipating the person's return. If the owner doesn't reappear in what the dog perceives as a reasonable length of time, the dog feels compelled to go seek out that person.

A Worker First and Foremost

Rottweiler owners cannot be reminded often enough that this dog was developed to work; he was bred to be a take-charge dog and is so to this day. Owners who begin their relationship with a puppy by letting that cute little darling sleep on their bed may later find themselves challenged

Young Rottweilers can be quite rowdy.

by that larger, older dog who now perceives the bed as his and suggests the owner should sleep elsewhere.

Rottweilers are usually demonstrably affectionate; in some instances this may progress to undesirable possessiveness. Proper discipline will prevent this behavior from happening. Remember, the primary definition of discipline is *training*, not punishment. Beneath the surface of the character of many Rottweilers is a desire to dominate. This trait can be expressed subtly—constant pawing to demand your attention, beginning boisterous play if you pick up the telephone, whining or barking if you have a conversation with someone. Other Rottweilers display their will to dominate in a more confrontational manner—they may growl if you walk by their food bowl (full or empty) or a favorite toy. Address these problems at an early age; otherwise, they may become insurmountable.

Wrestling and roughhousing, especially on the floor at the dog's level, can make dominance traits escalate. Most women who have Rottweilers have no inclination to indulge in such antics. However, many men, on seeing a large, powerful animal (especially a male dog), seem to have an almost uncontrollable urge to get physical and have a man-to-man face-off. This challenge is not a good idea, even with your own Rottweiler.

CHARACTERISTICS OF THE ROTTWEILER

territorial

playful

strong prey drive

pushy

loving with family, aloof with strangers

needs to have a "job"

By Nature, Somewhat Aloof

Somehow, in the past few years, the idea has become implanted in the minds of many (dog owners, trainers, veterinarians, etc.) that *all* dogs should accept *all* actions from *all* people. This does not describe the Rottweiler. The loving manner this breed displays to its family does not always extend to outsiders. Of course, any dog should be trained to submit to the examination of a veterinarian (or anyone designated by the owner). However, the Rottweiler is not inclined to permit familiarity by outsiders. Those who attempt it may wish they hadn't.

It's not uncommon for a Rottweiler to object to being rolled over on its back, even as a puppy. Instinct tells the dog that this is a submissive, vulnerable position. Most dogs can be conditioned to accept this, albeit sometimes with poor grace. I have known a few who seemed to say flat out, "No, you'll have to kill me first." If that happens, you must use your superior human intellect, and find a way to examine the dog's underside when necessary. Have the dog stand on a table, or place its front paws on something high, so you can look underneath.

Give Your Dog a Job

The Rottweiler possesses great intelligence. Owners are obliged to utilize that intelligence by interacting with the dog. With proper training and guidance, the Rottweiler will be very obedient; however, he was bred to make independent decisions and take independent action. As a dog bred for hard work, the healthy, well-conditioned Rottweiler has boundless energy and stamina (except in hot weather). He will be happier and more content if he has a few simple jobs to do. Carrying your packages, mail or newspaper will afford him great pleasure. It is not by happenstance that the Rottweiler has risen to the number two position in popularity of all registered dogs. Nor is the reason that all Rottweiler owners acquired the dog as a guardian. The fact of the matter is that Rottweilers are *fun* dogs and are ready to be your partner in almost any activity.

However, this breed is not suitable for casual ownership. Great responsibility and liability can be involved when you share your life with a Rottweiler. If the dog will be left unattended for hours, if you do not have a securely fenced yard where your Rottweiler may safely have

Rottweilers are very playful.

some freedom of movement, if you are too busy or too lazy to devote sufficient time to properly rear and train the dog, if you are too permissive to be a disciplinarian, then you would be wise to select another breed, one requiring less effort on your part.

Of all the adjectives I have heard applied to the Rottweiler, the one that offends me most is "stubborn." Any dog that can be taught to perform the many and varied functions the Rottweiler can is not stubborn. In cases where the Rottweiler is not learning to perform as required, proper motivation may be lacking. Assuming the attitude of a drill sergeant doesn't impress the Rottweiler. He is not a willing slave but is a most congenial and affable partner. Perhaps it's simply semantics. I have found that most owners who label their dogs stubborn do not mean to imply that the dog is deliberately obstinate or resistant to   more often, the word *determined* better describes their problem. For example, it's easier to teach a Rottweiler to do something it doesn't find to its liking than it is to suppress behavior that it's crazy about but you're not.

I must admit, many Rottweilers are born thieves and take great delight in acquiring their treasures. Once when I was away from home with my dogs, a neighbor kindly put a UPS package on my front step. When I returned home, I entered from the rear, letting the dogs into their yard. A couple of hours later I went outside to find the box in their doghouse, plastic packing peanuts scattered all over. The box had been torn open, then shredded; each item (and they were all wrapped separately) had been removed and deposited in one corner of the doghouse, unharmed. A female I had rescued from an unsuitable home was a skilled thief. I noticed one day that her bed looked very lumpy; hidden under it were fourteen shoes! Thievery does not indicate any lapse of morals in the Rottweiler—such traits don't exist in dogs. However, to prevent the dog from stealing something that may be damaging to him or distressful to you, it's best to employ the "ounce of prevention" rule.

You must at all times display the attitude of a leader.

Many Rottweilers welcome the challenge of a closed door—cupboard, closet, refrigerator, what have you. If you have other dogs or very small children, Rottweilers will be quick to take advantage of this unexpected access to food and forbidden articles. Another peculiarity of this breed, shared alike by males and females, is the propensity to roll on things. Of course, it's not uncommon for dogs of any breed to roll in carrion and other disgusting things, and some Rottweilers do this with great gusto. What I mean is rolling on objects—a ball, a washcloth, a chew toy, discarded clothing—anything may prompt them to fling themselves on it and have a good roll.

Be Your Rottweiler's Leader

With a dog of such incredible strength of body and will, it is imperative that the owner be the dog's leader. It's not enough to say, "You dog, me human—I'm the boss." If the dog does not believe you're the boss, you're not. You must at all times display the attitude and presence of a leader. This certainly does not mean brutality in training, nor does it mean shouting and keeping the dog subdued and fearful. It means that in your heart of hearts there must be no doubt that you are fully capable of controlling this animal. Even then, the dog may be prepared to disagree with you. If being a leader is not your strong suit, a Rottweiler is not the dog for you.

Rottweilers and water seem to go together—from the puppy that dabbles its front feet in the water bucket to the dog that hurls itself from the bank into deep water. It's not uncommon to see Rottweilers that actually retrieve objects from the bottom of a ten-foot pool.

In warm weather, Rottweilers greatly appreciate a dip in cool water, even if it's only a small wading pool. At the same time, some Rottweilers will walk a mile out of their way to avoid stepping into an inch-deep puddle! If introduced to the joy of water early and gently, the Rottweiler will usually take to it like the proverbial duck to water.

Rottweilers are on record as having saved people from burning buildings, car wrecks, swift rivers, earthquakes and landslides; their ability to respond to danger has earned them the nickname of the "good deed dog."

MORE INFORMATION ON ROTTWEILERS

NATIONAL BREED CLUB

American Rottweiler Club
Doreen LePage, Secretary
960 South Main Street
Pascoag, RI 02859

The club can give you information on all aspects of the breed, including the names and addresses of breed, obedience and herding clubs in your area. Inquire about membership.

BOOKS

Brace, Andrew, ed. *The Ultimate Rottweiler.* New York: Howell Book House, 1995.

Elsden, Judy and Larry. *The Rottweiler Today.* New York: Howell Book House, 1992.

Freeman, Muriel. *The Complete Rottweiler.* New York: Howell Book House, 1984.

Kern, Kerry. *Rottweilers: A Complete Pet Owner's Manual.* Hauppauge, N.Y.: Barron's Educational Series, 1991.

MacPhail, Mary. *Pet Owner's Guide to the Rottweiler.* New York: Howell Book House, 1993.

Nicholas, Anna Katherine. *The Book of the Rottweiler.* Neptune, N.J.: TFH Publications, 1981.

Nicholas, Anna Katherine. *The World of Rottweilers.* Neptune, N.J.: TFH Publications, 1986.

Price, Les. *Rottweilers: An Owner's Companion.* New York: Howell Book House, 1981.

Stratton, Richard F. *The Rottweiler.* Neptune, N.J.: TFH Publications, 1985.

MAGAZINES

The ARC, A Publication of the American Rottweiler Club

Marilyn Piusz
339 CO Highway 106
Johnstown, NY 12095-9730

The Rottweiler Quarterly
GRQ Publications
3355 Conant Lane
Watsonville, CA 95076

VIDEOS

Rottweilers. The American Kennel Club.

Living
with a

part two

Rottweiler

chapter 4

Bringing your
Rottweiler
Home

Before bringing home your puppy or if you have a new dog, everyone in your family must agree on who is responsible for feeding the dog, taking the puppy on potty breaks, walking the puppy and so forth. It's unrealistic to expect children, no matter how responsible, to consistently meet the demands of a puppy.

You need to decide in which room the puppy is to sleep; you will have on hand a stainless-steel food pan and a medium-steel water bucket, one not too high or with too narrow an opening. Yes, you can use a heavy plastic one, although the puppy may use it as a teething ring. Most owners are inclined to keep the puppy in a kitchen or bathroom because these rooms are usually uncarpeted and accidents are easier to clean up. However, slick surfaces are extremely dangerous for large-breed puppies. The pups can't get any traction, and their legs slide away from their body, sometimes causing permanent damage to hip and elbow joints. In a breed that suffers from joint disorders, this is not a wise risk to take.

You should have a soft leash (not a chain!)—cotton webbing is suitable and inexpensive. Flexi-leads (a handle with a long retractable line) are great for puppies because they eliminate the problem of leashes getting tangled in legs. They are good for walking dogs but totally unsuitable for training. In addition, you will need a flat, buckle collar—one that is adjustable, to allow for growth. You should always be able to insert two fingers between the animal's neck and the collar.

Using a Crate—It's Not Cruel

No matter what your past history is regarding dogs, let yourself be guided by the experts, most of whom recommend a crate for puppy rearing. Many pet owners shun this idea, visualizing the crate as a prison. This perception is *not* accurate. Puppies, like children, need a safe environment. No one sees anything wrong with placing a very young child in a playpen for the safety of the child. When you think *puppy*, think "baby." When you think *crate*, think "playpen." Puppies that are crate trained look on the crate as their den, their refuge, their "safe" place. Properly implemented (never used as punishment), the crate becomes a haven for the puppy, who will frequently retire to it voluntarily when in need of a nap or some quiet time. Many continue the practice after maturity.

Puppies should be crated for sleeping and when their owners are occupied elsewhere and cannot give them undivided attention. That way the puppies cannot chew on electrical cords, the furniture, carpeting or houseplants, any of which can prove fatal. Neither can they leave you little "gifts" behind the couch. Several manufacturers offer crates made of extruded plastic

PUPPY ESSENTIALS

Your new puppy will need:

food bowl

water bowl

collar

leash

I.D. tag

bed

crate

toys

grooming supplies

with a small opening on the top of each side covered by wire mesh and a wire door. Such crates are approved by the federal government for shipping dogs by air. Many prefer not to use this type for several reasons. One, air circulation is minimal, and the plastic retains heat. Two, the bottom is uneven; something must be inserted to prevent discomfort to the dog. Three, the crate must usually be disassembled before it can fit through the average car door. My choice is an all-wire crate of sufficiently heavy gauge wire to be suitable for an adult Rottweiler. The dog has maximum air circulation and visibility in all directions. To eliminate bright light or distractions, the crate may be covered. Most such crates are available in easily collapsible form, which makes them quite portable and easy to store. They are available in many attractive finishes.

A tiny puppy does not require the size crate it will need when mature. However, to avoid purchasing different sized crates, purchase a large one, suitable for an adult, then insert a piece of smooth plywood between the wires vertically, cutting the space about in half. Dogs do not like to soil their sleeping quarters—if the puppy's space is restricted, it quickly learns to alert you when it needs to eliminate. If too large a space is provided, the puppy will eliminate at the end of the crate, farthest from its bed, increasing the time and difficulty of housetraining.

Wire crates are furnished with a removable metal tray insert for the floor. These are cold, hard and slippery. Your inclination will be to place a soft blanket inside. However, most puppies chew; when teething (at about four and one-half months and often until age two), the puppy will be inclined to chew everything in sight, including the blanket. In addition to causing expensive replacements, if the bedding is ingested, the puppy may not be able to pass it and must then be treated by your veterinarian—possibly requiring surgery. One solution is a piece of masonite (plywood is too slippery), cut to fit the bottom of the crate; turn it rough-side-out, so the dog is not on a slippery surface. Superior to this but slightly more expensive are heavy-duty plastic interlocking tiles, which the puppy cannot chew and which permit water to drain. They have a nonskid surface, are easily cleaned off by hosing, are extremely durable and well worth the price.

Crates Are Safe Havens

A man once visited me with his fifteen-month-old Rottweiler. He had traveled a great distance for some training instruction from me and had borrowed his wife's new car to make the trip. He left the dog, uncrated, in the car while we sat in the house and drank coffee. He explained that he had no need of a crate because his dog never did anything destructive. When we walked out to his car, we found the head-liner hanging in shreds, the upholstery on either side torn out and the backseat in rags. The damage to the car was secondary; what concerned us was the possibility that the dog might have swallowed some tacks or pieces of foam rubber. The whole incident necessitated an expensive trip to the vet, not to mention repair of the vehicle. I can only imagine the reaction of the man's wife. In the best interests of the puppy, your house, your belongings—and your state of mind—crate train your puppy. Better safe than sorry.

After he outgrows the chewing stage, give your puppy a real bed. Beds are available in almost every size, shape and color. Many of them have cedar filling, which cuts down on odor and discourages external parasites; they may also have a foam rubber pad. Usually the outside cover zips off for easy washing. Make certain that the soap or detergent is nontoxic, and rinse the bed three or four times in clear water to totally flush the detergent from it. Most people place the bed on the floor in a corner of the room. In cold weather there is usually an unpleasant draft at floor level. Although dogs may withstand

Puppies, like children, need safe environments.

39

severe drops of temperature, they do not tolerate drafts and dampness well, and puppies need to be kept warm. I keep my dog beds raised about six inches off the floor.

HOUSEHOLD DANGERS

Curious puppies and inquisitive dogs get into trouble not because they are bad, but simply because they want to investigate the world around them. It's our job to protect our dogs from harmful substances, like the following:

IN THE HOUSE

cleaners, especially pine oil

perfumes, colognes, aftershaves

medications, vitamins

office and craft supplies

electric cords

chicken or turkey bones

chocolate

some house and garden plants, like ivy, oleander and poinsettia

IN THE GARAGE

Antifreeze

garden supplies, like snail and slug bait, pesticides, fertilizers, mouse and rat poisons

Toys and Games

Puppies (and most adult Rottweilers) need toys and playthings, but owners can get excessive with what they give them. A puppy with a choice of many toys may go from one toy to the another, never actually playing with any of them. It's best to have only two or three toys available at any given time. New toys can be introduced now and then, but some of the more familiar ones should then be removed, so there are never too many available. Hard rubber chew toys are suitable, and tug toys are fine provided they are made of cotton or hard rubber. Never jerk or shake an object the puppy has in its mouth—doing so can cause damage to teeth and jaws. Let the puppy do the shaking and pulling—you simply hold on.

If your puppy is overly aggressive, playing tug-of-war can provoke an undesirable reaction. Puppies should always win the game but should also be taught to give up the object on command. Many breeders advance the theory that tugging games can ruin the puppy's "bite," that is, how the teeth mesh. Since the lower jaw continues growing after the upper jaw has stopped, it seems like a reasonable premise, although I know of no actual proof of this and have never had it happen to any of my dogs. However, you must decide for yourself if you wish to take the risk.

Teasing a puppy or adult Rottweiler with toys or food is a cruel form of entertainment for you and frustrating for the dog. It can also lead to unacceptable behavior. Some of the toys your caring heart might encourage you to buy are extremely hazardous to puppies and adult dogs alike. Rawhide chews usually turn into a soggy mass and are then swallowed. They can block the throat, the intestine and the bowel. Cow hooves and horns as well as antlers are attractive to dogs—at best, your dog will have a severe stomach ache, at worst, a punctured intestine. The first thing a dog usually does with a squeaky toy is remove the squeaker and swallow it. It may pass—and it may not.

Any ball that's small enough to be swallowed probably will be. If it lodges in the windpipe, chances are you can't get help quickly enough to save the dog's life. Particularly dangerous are hard rubber handballs. Even that all-time favorite, the tennis ball, can be deadly. Many dogs have a tendency to compress the ball in their mouths, enjoying the slight resistance. If they compress it enough, even accidentally, then inhale, the ball goes down the throat. Tennis balls are available with a twelve-inch nylon rope through the center. This decreases the resistance of the ball and also makes it easier to grab the rope if the dog does gulp the ball. It's nicer for you because you can throw it by the rope instead of grasping a ball slimy with dog saliva. Wash the tennis ball thoroughly before you use it because many are colored with a dye that may be injurious to the dog. Use it only as a throw toy; don't permit the dog to play with it unattended.

Dogs usually like soft vinyl toys but should only be allowed to have them when interacting with their owners. Left to its own devices, the dog will chew and swallow such toys. For the Rottweiler that is really "ball happy," the best choice is a ball made of what is called "plantation rubber." Get one larger than a tennis ball; this will be too large and hard for him to apply sufficient pressure for serious chewing. It will last long and has tremendous bounce even on soft ground.

Not Fancy, But Fun

Puppies, like children, will sometimes leave their expensive toys and opt to play with more mundane objects. Mine have always been delighted with gallon-sized plastic milk jugs. I rinse them thoroughly, remove the label, and the dogs play with them by the hour. They take a special delight in flattening the jug; then, using it as a sort of skid, they push it all over the yard with stiffened forelegs, roaring their pleasure aloud.

*An older
Rottweiler
makes a fine
friend, too.*

Ordinary rope can be dangerous to puppies; they are inclined to bite off segments of varying lengths and swallow them. This item is another that frequently must be removed surgically. Outdoor toys can include "boomer" balls (ten-inch-diameter polystyrene balls), which are virtually indestructable and a great workout for the dog. I always have two or three barrels in the dog yard—some plastic, some metal. The males usually try to get a shoulder under it and toss it—the females usually put their front paws on it and roll it back and forth. Both activities are usually accompanied by much play growling and barking.

Remember, simply because an item is advertised and sold as a toy for pets does not insure that it is safe for pets. Having puppy proofed your house (made sure that your Rottweiler does not have access to toxic substances stored under kitchen or bathroom sinks, made certain that electrical cords are not reachable and therefore chewable, etc.) and provided a securely fenced yard free of debris, garbage or trash, you may feel your Rottweiler is safe. Unfortunately, the modern world is a hostile environment, and your puppy is still in danger from everyday items. Many houseplants are toxic to dogs— poinsettia, chrysanthemum, ivy, creeping Charlie, philodendron and many more. Toxic outdoor plants include delphinium, daffodil and wisteria; dangerous trees and shrubs are horse chestnut, English holly, mock orange, privet and oleander, among others.

Rest and Relaxation

Sleep and rest are very important to the Rottweiler. Dogs are so engineered that they can go from a dead sleep to a dead run in nothing flat, but if no external stimulus is provided, some dogs will sleep two-thirds of the day. A puppy given ample opportunity for naps will be happier and better adjusted than the one that does not get adequate rest. When puppies need to rest, they are best left alone. Low background music or the television may be soothing (it also drowns out other noises); however, if there is loud conversation or children shouting and playing, it may be difficult for the puppy to rest. Many puppies need to wind down after stimulating activity. A little crate time with one favorite toy will usually slow them down so that eventually they sleep.

Exercise Is Essential

Of equal importance is exercise. Puppies need frequent periods of activity during the day, interspersed with naps. Puppies should not be dragged along on walks too long for their endurance or at a speed too fast for their short legs. Flights of stairs are hazardous to young joints and muscles; jumping off furniture (where they shouldn't be in the first place) can cause serious damage to legs and spine. Interacting with you and their toys in the yard when the weather is pleasant, indoors when the weather is bad, will provide all the exercise a very young puppy needs.

As it matures, your puppy will tolerate (and require) longer walks and greater activity for longer periods. The adult Rottweiler will enjoy two or three fairly long walks a day, in addition to some free time in a reasonably large, fenced yard. However, this exercise is not sufficient to keep it in good shape. Fifteen or twenty minutes a day vigorously chasing a ball, particularly uphill, will keep your Rottweiler fit. Your dog is not a tree—you can't "plant" it in the backyard, feed and water it and expect it to flourish. Rottweilers require lots of personal attention and are the worse for not receiving it.

Rottweilers require lots of personal attention.

Dogs receive much information from the scents they encounter. A dog can sniff the grass and determine what other dog passed there, how long ago, its sex and various other information of no interest to you. This sniffing, in addition to bringing great joy, also stimulates the dog to urinate and defecate. Responsible owners carry a plastic bag in which to scoop up droppings. It's inconsiderate to let your Rottweiler make deposits on a neighbor's lawn or in a public park. Unfortunately, many diseases are transmitted through urine, feces and saliva deposited by infected dogs.

Being a Good Canine Neighbor

As a caring owner, you know your Rottweiler should not run loose both for its own sake and for the sake of the community. Dogs permitted to roam uncontrolled are in constant danger from traffic, disease and attack by other animals and people. They degrade the quality of urban, suburban and rural life and can create dangerous hostility against their owners as well as themselves. If taking a sashay through the neighborhood, your Rottweiler can be neither companion nor protector to you; your dog should either be indoors, safely confined behind a fence or walking with you on leash. Of course, no dog should have to live its life at the end of a chain. Rottweilers that are forced to do so often become mindlessly aggressive or totally indifferent to their surroundings, including humans.

Despite all precautions, accidents do happen and dogs become lost, stray or are stolen. All dogs should wear a flat collar (never a slip or choke collar) with proper identification. However, collars can be removed by the dog, other dogs, humans or by simply getting caught on something. Describing your Rottweiler as black and tan is not being very specific. As positive proof of ownership, many people tattoo their dogs. Tattooing is a relatively painless procedure, and it's permanent.

If you plan to make your Rottweiler an outside dog with no house privileges, you should get another breed. Rottweilers don't thrive in a kennel environment, nor can your Rottweiler form a bond with you if left alone. Dogs are creatures of habit; as such, a schedule is very important to their development. To have a dog whose eating, sleeping and eliminating requirements are compatible with your schedule, *adhere to a routine,* one based on the capability of the dog's age level. Doing the same thing in the same manner at approximately the same time each day determines the speed with which the puppy is housetrained, provides the foundation for making the dog a consistent eater rather than a picky one and enables the puppy to adjust to occasionally being alone. A schedule gives your dog a sense of security.

Puppies do love to chew!

Making a Rottweiler Right for You

This book has so far addressed caring for the Rottweiler puppy. But what if you don't have the time to properly raise a puppy but still would like to have a Rottweiler share your life? All the foregoing requirements and cautions apply, plus a few more. If you have never previously owned a Rottweiler and have decided on an adult, I strongly urge that you select a female.

They are every bit as enjoyable and protective as the male but less dominant or inclined to challenge your authority. The American Rottweiler Club can supply you with information regarding area clubs and individuals who do rescue work for the Rottweiler; they occasionally have adult dogs that, through no fault of the dog, need to be placed in a new home. Usually, these dogs will have been medically evaluated and temperament tested before they are released.

Puppies are inquisitive and playful.

Unfortunately, many animal shelters have adult Rottweilers impounded. It's best to have the advice of an experienced dog person before assuming responsibility for a large dog whose background is unknown to you. Many dogs are in shelters because an owner, for whatever reason, found the dog impossible or dangerous to live with. Many Rottweilers adopted from dog pounds, nevertheless, turn out to be wonderful additions to the family. There are, however, many instances of Rottweilers that have never received proper socialization, affection and training. Such dogs usually find it difficult to adjust to a family, although they may do well with a single owner. Even a Rottweiler with a good background may feel ill at ease in new surroundings with strangers and have a lapse of manners. Be tolerant and understanding, and give the dog ample opportunity to relieve itself outdoors. Adult or puppy, time and effort are necessary to establish rapport and develop a good relationship.

chapter 5

Feeding
your
Rottweiler

When the topic of diet arises in any group of dog owners, from professionals to the rankest amateurs, there will be as many diverse opinions as there are people present, and not all those opinions have validity. We have learned much in recent years about what is beneficial in a dog's diet and what is  not. Food items that people swore by ten years ago have been found to be less than wonderful for the dog, and frequently detrimental to its overall health. Despite all the knowledge gained, there are some who will not concede that there might be a better way.

Types of Dog Foods

Dog foods are available in several forms—dry (kibble), canned or semimoist. Kibble is the preferred form not only because of economy or ease of preparation, but also because the other forms do not meet the dietary needs of the Rottweiler, plus they may contain more than one injurious ingredient. Semimoist foods are usually loaded with salt, sugar and artificial coloring (frequently Red 2K dye is used, to which many dogs are extremely sensitive). It is not well balanced and does not provide the nutrition your Rottweiler needs. Canned foods frequently have poor-quality cereal and, according to most labels, are about 75 percent moisture. If the label indicates the presence of meat, determine what the source of the meat is.

Plenty of water is as important as the right food.

Some canned foods are quite good (and expensive) and may provide an adequate diet for a small dog. They are not recommended for a Rottweiler. If you are feeding a good-quality kibble and preparing it properly, there is no need to add canned food (or anything else) to induce the dog to eat. A healthy dog with adequate exercise that has not been taught bad eating habits will devour food. A well-balanced, completely nutritious dry kibble, free of artificial preservatives, is the preferred choice of most knowledgeable dog owners. *Do not choose your Rottweiler's kibble casually, buying whatever is on sale or convenient.* Many foods sold in supermarkets include lots of salt and sugar, artificial flavor and color, sweepings from the floor and trash byproducts from meat packers, which may include feathers, fur and feet.

Reading Labels

Learn to be a label reader. Does the label indicate a suitable protein content? What is the source of the protein? If it's vegetable, it will be of less benefit to your dog because dogs do not assimilate vegetable protein well. Too much protein is as bad as not enough. Is a natural preservative present to keep the ingredients fresh, or is it chemically preserved by something that gives the product a shelf life longer than the dog's life span? Puppies require double the amount of nutrients required by adults, on the basis of units of body weight.

The proper ratio of calcium and phosphorous must be maintained; this ratio is one of the reasons that owners should not formulate their own dog food at home. Even if you are an avid label reader, there is not sufficient information on a dog food label to enable you to compare one food with another. Most dog food manufacturers will send you a breakdown of the ingredients, but this may be couched in language difficult to understand without a background in chemistry or nutrition.

A few simple facts will enable you to make a better choice: (1) Federal law dictates what can be written on the label. The first four ingredients listed are the primary ones, in the order listed. (2) You can't even buy hot dogs for twenty cents per pound; there's no reason you should expect to buy a good-quality dog food for that price. Depending on where you live in relation to where the food is produced (freight accounts for a large part of the price—often as much as a third), a good-quality kibble will run anywhere from sixty cents to eighty cents per pound, twenty-four dollars to thirty-two dollars per forty-pound bag. (3) You will feed less of a good-quality food. Being well balanced and totally nutritious, it satisfies the dog's appetite. Dogs fed on cheap food are

> ### HOW MANY MEALS A DAY?
>
> Individual dogs vary in how much they should eat to maintain a desired body weight—not too fat, but not too thin. Puppies need several meals a day, while older dogs may need only one. Determine how much food keeps your adult dog looking and feeling her best. Then decide how many meals you want to feed with that amount. Like us, most dogs love to eat, and offering two meals a day is more enjoyable for them. If you're worried about overfeeding, make sure you measure correctly and abstain from adding tidbits to the meals.
>
> Whether you feed one or two meals, only leave your dog's food out for the amount of time it takes her to eat it—10 minutes, for example. Freefeeding (when food is available any time) and leisurely meals encourage picky eating. Don't worry if your dog doesn't finish all her dinner in the allotted time. She'll learn she should.

frequently overweight and undernourished. (4) With a good-quality food you will have less cleanup of stools as well as easier cleanup. Poor-quality protein will pass through a dog's intestinal tract without being used; the stools will be loose or very soft. Cheaper foods often produce a most unpleasant odor in the stools. Stools should be firm (not hard) and well formed. Many think that foods containing soy bean, in any form, can lead to bloat and subsequent stomach torsion. The bottom line is *there is no one best food*. What one dog may thrive on, another cannot utilize. You will have many choices in the price range referred to above.

Feeding Your Puppy

If you're feeding a puppy (under six months of age), select one of the quality foods formulated specifically for puppies. If normal and healthy, the puppy will not need additives or supplements. To add these upsets the balance of the food you have chosen and can cause serious bone disorders. Puppies need to be fed small amounts, three or four times daily. The rate of growth in a breed like the Rottweiler is tremendous, from possibly three-quarters of a pound at birth to possibly 100 pounds at one year. Puppies need a food that meets the demands of their bodies but does not encourage or promote excessive early growth. For this reason, at approximately five months of age, I start switching my puppies to an adult formula and by six months the transition is complete.

Feeding Your Adult

Adult dogs need an adult maintenance diet, based on normal activity. There are some who feel that overloading the stomach by feeding one large meal per day is risking bloat and opt to feed adults twice a day. Intake can vary from dog to dog and with varying conditions such as warm weather, decreased activity and so forth. Older dogs have lower caloric requirements; if the dog is really a dedicated eater, it is better to feed the usual amount of a food lower in calories than to simply reduce the amount of a higher calorie food. If you teach your dog to honor a sit–stay command and not dive into the food pan until you speak the magic word, you will have taken a giant stride toward establishing your supremacy in the dog's mind.

The recommended feeding amounts listed on the bags of most dog foods are not realistic. For example, I feed a lamb and rice–based kibble of good quality. My dogs are considerably more active than the average pet. The manufacturer recommends feeding 4¾ to 5¾ cups for a dog of 80 to 100 pounds. My two-and-a-half-year-old male, not quite mature, weighs 120 pounds and keeps in good condition on only 4 cups per day, plus two nourishing biscuits. My seven-year-old bitch, extremely active, weighs in at 75–80 pounds and stays fit on less than 2 cups per day. The recommended amount is 3 to 4 cups. I have seen as many as 12 cups recommended by some of the cheaper brands. This is an incredible volume of food to load in the dog's stomach; even if you feed twice a day, with that amount of food the dog's digestive system would be almost constantly at work.

Obesity and loose, frequent stools are only two of the results of overfeeding. Probably the worst thing an owner can do is to let the dog be a "self-feeder," that is, to place a week's supply of dry food in a pan, and let the dog eat at will. The dog's appetite is one of the best indicators of its health; if the dog has free choice, by the time you are aware of a problem, the situation may have deteriorated seriously. Feeding free

HOW TO READ THE DOG FOOD LABEL

With so many choices on the market, how can you be sure you are feeding the right food for your dog? The information is all there on the label—if you know what you're looking for.

Look for the nutritional claim right up top. Is the food "100% nutritionally complete"? If so, it's for nearly all life stages; "growth and maintenance," on the other hand, is for early development; puppy foods are marked as such, as are foods for senior dogs.

Ingredients are listed in descending order by weight. The first three or four ingredients will tell you the bulk of what the food contains. Look for the highest-quality ingredients, like meats and grains, to be among them.

The Guaranteed Analysis tells you what levels of protein, fat, fiber and moisture are in the food, in that order. While these numbers are meaningful, they won't tell you much about the quality of the food. Nutritional value is in the dry matter, not the moisture content.

In many ways, seeing is believing. If your dog has bright eyes, a shiny coat, a good appetite and a good energy level, chances are his diet's fine. Your dog's breeder and your veterinarian are good sources of advice if you're still confused.

choice is unsanitary: dirty flies swarm on the food, ants and other insects crawl into it and the dog salivates in it, causing the food to sour. It drastically reduces your importance in the eyes of the dog. It is a lazy person's solution to what should be a much-anticipated daily event.

Know How Much You're Feeding

Be sure each day to measure the amount you feed your Rottweiler, using a simple measuring cup to scoop it out of the bag. If your dog has a problem and has to be taken to the veterinarian, you may be asked, "How much does your dog eat each day?" It sounds really stupid to respond by saying, "He gets three blue bowls full." It gives the vet no information because no one knows what size your blue bowl is. Learn to feed specific amounts.

*Dogs know
when it's
dinnertime.*

All dry food expands when moisture is added, whether the moisture is added by you or the dog's stomach. If the food expands inside the dog's stomach, there's a strong possibility it will induce bloat. Make the simple test of leaving one kibble in a bowl of water overnight; the size to which it expands may surprise you. Most nutritionists and veterinarian colleges recommend that warm water be liberally added to the food until it's almost soupy; stir, then let stand for at least fifteen minutes (more for some foods); stir again before feeding. Food should be served at room temperature, never too cold or too hot, and only after all the liquid has been absorbed. A healthy Rottweiler, puppy or adult, should be an eager eater. Puppies lose their concentration easily, so it's best to feed them in a restricted space. If the dog has not cleaned up the food in a reasonable amount of time (roughly fifteen minutes), remove the pan and refrigerate the food until the next scheduled feeding. If poor appetite persists, visit your veterinarian.

Your Rottweiler should be kept inactive for at least one-half hour before eating and one hour after eating. Feed in a quiet area, free from distraction and interruption. Food pans should be picked up as soon as the dog is finished, and cleaned thoroughly before the next use. As with all dogs, the Rottweiler's digestive system is that of a carnivore, as are its teeth and method of eating. Whether wild canine or domestic dog, the teeth are used in the same fashion—the incisors for biting and hygiene, the canines for the seizing and tearing of food and the molars for shearing of soft tissue and bones. In its natural habitat the wild dog will gnaw pieces of meat off a carcass with its large back molars, then gulp down the smaller pieces whole. Do not be concerned if your dog gulps its food—it's a natural tendency.

Adding Extras

Whether or not to feed table scraps is controversial. Most dog experts agree they should be avoided; they do upset the balance of the food you have specifically chosen for the dog and can cause upset of the digestive system. Having said that, it must be acknowledged that most dog owners are tempted from time to time to add something to their Rottweiler's food, "just because."

Okay, so you're occasionally going to add some table scraps. Make certain that this does *not* include pastry, candy, potatoes, greasy food and so forth. Table scraps should *never* constitute more than 25 percent of the dog's diet at any given meal. If you indulge your Rottweiler with meat scraps from dinner, be certain to remove the fat. Holiday dinners featuring roasted stuffed poultry can be disastrous events for your Rottweiler if it's fed pieces of skin. These are not only usually heavily seasoned but resemble rubber in consistency. Stuffing, no matter how delectable to your palate, is bad for the dog.

Most legumes (like the pea) cannot be digested by the dog, although one dog food company adds them in whole, dried form. Most cereal grains if properly prepared and cooked by the dog food manufacturers are fine for dogs. Some vegetables are relished by dogs (tomatoes, for example) and, in moderation, will have no ill effects. Others (like cabbage) are indigestible and may cause flatulence. Many Rottweilers thoroughly enjoy fruit—grapes, bananas and so forth; however, be very wary of fruits containing pits, especially apricots, peaches and cherries. The pits of these fruits contain cyanide. Even pits that don't contain any toxin should be kept from the dog because they can cause blockage. Many Rottweilers will happily munch on any kind of melon. As long as they are eating the meat of the melon there is no problem; however, rinds of any melon are indigestible and usually get hung up in the bowel instead of being passed. Kernels of corn are completely indigestible but, finely ground, can be readily assimilated. Never permit a dog to have a corn cob—he cannot digest it, and it frequently acts as an effective plug.

Whole cow's milk frequently causes gas or diarrhea. It is not needed by weaned puppies or adults. No matter—some people feel better if they add it to the dog food. If you are one of those people, dilute the milk with water. Bacon grease or other

TYPES OF FOODS/TREATS

There are three types of commercially available dog food—dry, canned and semimoist—and a huge assortment of treats (lucky dogs!) to feed your dog. Which should you choose?

Dry and canned foods contain similar ingredients. The primary difference between them is their moisture content. The moisture is not just water. It's blood and broth, too, the very things that dogs adore. So while canned food is more palatable, dry food is more economical, convenient and effective in controlling tartar buildup. Most owners feed a 25% canned/75% dry diet to give their dogs the benefit of both. Just be sure your dog is getting the nutrition he needs (you and your veterinarian can determine this).

Semimoist foods have the flavor dogs love and the convenience owners want. However, they tend to contain excessive amounts of artificial colors and preservatives.

Dog treats come in every size, shape and flavor imaginable, from organic cookies shaped like postmen to beefy chew sticks. Dogs seem to love them all, so enjoy the variety. Just be sure not to overindulge your dog. Factor treats into her regular meal sizes.

meat drippings certainly add flavor and, for the dog that is working hard or exposed to severe cold, can be beneficial. For the average pet, they simply produce loose stools. As a general rule, avoid pork altogether.

Meat Treats and Bones

The household pet is not called on to perform feats of endurance and stamina; it's not necessary to add meat to a well-balanced kibble, but if you insist on doing so, the meat should be cooked, never fed raw. Probably you know that dogs should never receive any kind of poultry bone, but do you know that this rule also applies to *all* steak and chop bones, rib and neck bones and fish bones? The popular belief is that such bones get stuck in a dog's throat, but this is a small part of the potential danger. Long after the dog has crunched and swallowed the bone, it can cause damage by puncturing the intestine or impacting the anal glands. In other words, dogs should not have any real bone except a big beef knuckle bone, and the only pur-

> **TO SUPPLEMENT OR NOT TO SUPPLEMENT?**
>
> If you're feeding your dog a diet that's correct for her developmental stage and she's alert, healthy-looking and neither over- nor underweight, you don't need to add supplements. These include table scraps as well as vitamins and minerals. In fact, a growing puppy is in danger of developing musculoskeletal disorders by oversupplementation. If you have any concerns about the nutritional quality of the food you're feeding, discuss them with your veterinarian.

pose this serves is for personal enjoyment and polishing the teeth. I used to give knuckle bones to my dogs, but most of them spent all their time guarding it—one foot holding it down and growling at anything that even looked at it, including birds. The bones got dirt on them and grease on the dog's foot, and they attracted wild bees and ants, so I stopped.

Foods to Avoid

Spicy foods (like pizza or chili) play havoc with the Rottweiler's digestive system. Eggs are a good source of protein for both puppy and adult but must be cooked. Dogs cannot assimilate the raw egg white. Never feed a whole cooked egg—it may lodge in the dog's windpipe. Avoid commercial canine food enhancers. They consist of artificial colors and flavors and water. A normal, healthy Rottweiler should not have to be coaxed or duped into eating palatable food. Treats are relished by your Rottweiler—make certain they are appropriate. Avoid multicolored or artificially flavored biscuits. Select a good-quality biscuit (with no soybean or wheat middlings), sufficiently hard to force the dog to chew it. *Never, ever* give your dog chocolate. Chocolate contains a substance called theobromine, which is highly toxic to dogs. Ingestion of even a small amount may prove fatal. Dogs don't need variety in their diet or to learn to beg for food, either from your hand or the table. The opposite is true. Find a quality kibble that your dog thrives on, and if you are wise, never introduce your dog to people food.

chapter 6

Grooming
your
Rottweiler

There is an old saying among breeders that good coat is "bred for, fed for and cared for." As with most old saws, there's a good deal of truth in it. Whether or not good coat was part of your Rottweiler's inheritance is beyond your control. However, you can do your best with what you have. The number-one rule is that the coat must look and feel clean and smell pleasant.

Giving Your Rottweiler a Bath

The bath: Most dogs with undercoats such as the Rottweiler's do not require frequent bathing. Generally, spring and autumn baths are sufficient unless the dog has rolled in something offensive or has gotten something on its coat that must be removed. Do not use human shampoos, even those formulated for babies. They tend to strip the natural oils from the dog's coat. I am loathe to apply toxic insecticides to my dogs, so I opt for a hypoallergenic, moisture-intensified conditioning shampoo called Nova Pearls. It leaves the coat glossy, does not dry it out and is safe for dogs and cats.

Very young puppies should not be bathed, but for all others, if it is absolutely necessary, the puppy should be kept in a very warm room until the coat is thoroughly dry, a period requiring several hours. If I'm bathing a youngster, I prefer to use the bathtub, first making sure that its bottom has a rubberized mat to give the dog secure footing.

I make certain that towels and shampoo are handy before starting, so I never have a reason to leave the tub while the dog is in it. Before getting the animal wet, plug its ears with wads of cotton and place a drop of mineral oil in each eye to prevent soap burn. Use a spray nozzle to

Regular grooming removes dead skin and hair, reducing shedding.

wet the dog, then lather and rinse the head, being careful to keep soap and water out of eyes and ears. After the head has been thoroughly rinsed, shampoo the rest of the dog. Rinsing is of critical importance; if any shampoo residue is left, it can seriously irritate the skin and dull the coat. Rinse at least twice until no trace of soap remains. Squeeze the hair, removing excess moisture, cover the dog with a towel and remove it from the tub. Do not let dogs jump into or out of tubs—they are usually too eager and may slip and injure themselves. Towel the dog vigorously, removing as much water as possible.

You will need to use several towels and possibly a dryer on an older puppy. For an adult dog, if it is a warm, sunny day, you might let the dog go out onto the lawn where it will shake itself vigorously and want to roll on the grass; both actions remove a lot of moisture. Dogs usually get the "galloping sillies" at this point and will run in huge circles. If they have access to flower gardens, they may attempt to roll in dirt. Repeat the toweling process with a dry towel. In very warm weather the dog may be left outside to dry. If there's a chill in the air, bring the dog indoors. Even inside a warm house, the dog may chill because its coat is wet. It helps if you teach your dog to submit to a blow dryer. It should always be kept on a low setting. Never use Lysol or any household disinfectant (including bleach), or lemon or vinegar as a rinse.

I have installed a hot water pipe to an outside faucet so that I can mix hot and cold water to a suitable temperature (hot enough to feel comfortable to your hand) and use the garden hose to bathe my dogs in good weather. Sometimes, the noise is scary for a very young puppy, so I wait until they are about six months old before introducing them to this method. During our dry, dusty summers, I frequently hose them off, omitting the shampoo. Rottweilers that obey the stand–stay command are easy to bathe.

Regular Brushing's a Must

Nothing beats regular brushing for keeping a coat in good condition; it also provides a wonderful opportunity to examine the dog for abnormal lesions, lumps, sore spots and so forth as well as giving you the chance to use obedience commands in a practical circumstance. A terrier mitt (i.e., a mitt that fits over your hand and is smooth on one side, with soft wire pins on the other) is ideal for a Rottweiler. Brushing should be a daily activity and is one that most dogs enjoy. After all, the dog is getting your undivided attention.

Just about the time you think you have a handle on this and it's all pretty easy comes the dreaded spring shed, when the Rottweiler loses its undercoat. At this point you may have to use several tools—brushes, combs and

GROOMING TOOLS

pin brush

slicker brush

flea comb

towel

matt rake

grooming glove

scissors

nail clippers

tooth-cleaning equipment

shampoo

conditioner

clippers

so forth. Some Rottweilers shed more than others. I have one bitch that I can brush thoroughly four or five times a day during her shedding time. At each session I remove enough hair to make a whole other dog, although there's never any visible hair loss when you look at her. Fortunately, this period is brief, perhaps a week or two. Dogs that spend their time mostly indoors, with alternate periods outdoors, frequently shed year round, although not to the extent they do in spring. Shedding is not regulated by temperature but by exposure to light. The more exposure to light, whether natural or artificial, the more shedding. There are many commercial dry shampoos that keep coats in good condition without bathing, or you may opt to use fuller's earth or cornstarch. When using dry shampoos you must brush against the lay of the hair down to the skin.

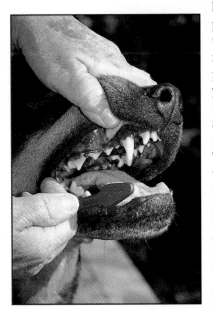

With practice, your dog will accept having its teeth brushed.

A Rottweiler's hair does not experience continuous growth; it grows for about five months, then rests. After that it dies, is shed, and the cycle begins again. Adult Rottweilers that spend a good deal of time on hard surfaces may develop callouses on bony pressure points, especially on elbows and hocks. These originate as simply a bare patch of skin from which the hair has been rubbed off by friction. The bare patch becomes a gray, thickened pad of wrinkled skin. It is more common in the heavier male and in dogs that are confined in concrete areas. Such a hairless area is unpleasing to the eye, and if left unattended and with no improvement in the surface on which the dog rests, the skin surface may break down, forming a running sore with drainage from the hair pores. It is extremely resistant to treatment. Prevention is quite easy—keep the dog off hard surfaces.

Part of my daily routine is to moisten a soft cloth with warm water and wipe eyes and muzzles and lips. Because my dogs do a lot of "fun biting on each other's neck," I also wipe this area every day; otherwise, they begin to smell. If for some reason you decide to take your Rottweiler to a professional groomer, emphasize that the whiskers should not be trimmed. These whiskers are not facial hair but are vibrassa (feelers) and are important to the dog. Except for perhaps that little point of hair at the tip of the Rottweiler's tail, they do not need trimming.

Taking Care of Toenails

Care of toenails (claws) is vital to the Rottweiler's general health. Nails that grow too long sometimes split, clear back to the base. More often, the dog will jam them against a hard surface, causing a nail to pop up at the base. This condition is extremely painful, and the nail must then be removed (ouch!), leaving the nail bed open to infection until covered by a new nail. Uncut dewclaws can and do grow in a circle, sometimes entering the pad. Puppies are frequently born without dewclaws on the hind legs; if not, they are removed when the puppy is a few days old. Many breeders prefer to leave the dewclaws on the front legs in the belief that it gives the dog greater dexterity when it uses its front feet. This is undoubtedly true; however, with dogs that are very active, the dewclaw can be ripped from its base. Because a small bone is involved, this accident can be quite painful.

Nails that are constantly too long cause dogs to alter their natural gait; they will bear their weight on the backs of the upper feet rather than on the pads as they should. This posture will eventually precipitate leg bone, shoulder and spinal discomfort. If uncorrected, the damage may be permanent. If you can hear your dog's claws click as it walks across a bare floor, they are too long. Puppies may be started off with a guillotine-type nail clipper, removing just the pointed tip. If you cut too much, you will cut the quick—the sensitive part containing nerves and blood vessels—causing pain and bleeding. A styptic will help to stop the bleeding. Causing pain will certainly make the dog reluctant to have its feet handled, so proceed cautiously.

There is no law that requires you to do all nails on all four feet at one time. With puppies it's best to do just one foot at a time. With my adult dogs, it takes about five minutes per dog. Even dogs who wear their nails short on hard surfaces frequently need pedicures because the nails are rough or uneven.

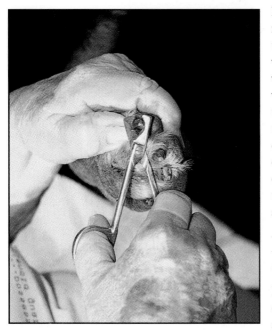

*Toenails
need regular
clipping.*

Ears are frequently repositories of dust that mixes with ear-wax and should be wiped out once a week with a wad of soft cotton. It's not necessary to put anything on the cotton. Examine the eyes and ears after the dog has had a run in tall grass; remove any seeds or foreign matter.

For All-Over Good Health

Probably because no one ever told them about the importance of regular inspection, most pet owners seldom get past the top of the head. However, to keep your dog in good health and catch problems before they become serious, make it a point to examine teeth, inside the mouth, under the tongue, eyes, ears, paws, under-carriage, penile sheath and testicles of the male, vulva of the female and area surrounding the anus. This inspection can be incorporated into your routine grooming.

Keeping your
Rottweiler
Healthy

"An ounce of prevention is worth a pound of cure," and this adage certainly applies to your Rottweiler's health. Most ethical breeders, out of necessity, inform themselves about simple routine procedures and learn to spot a problem in the making. The typical pet owner has neither the motivation nor background to acquire such extensive knowledge. However, being aware of potential difficulties enables you to seek veterinary care in a timely manner.

A Good Vet Goes a Long Way

Having a competent veterinarian who respects the animals under his care can greatly increase the well-being of your Rottweiler, as well as your enjoyment of the dog. It is no pleasure for the Rottweiler, the veterinarian or the owner to deal with a dog that is unruly. It's up to the owner to expose the puppy to frequent visits to the veterinarian even if no procedures are scheduled. A cookie now and then from the staff and the veterinarian plus the opportunity to become familiar with the intimidating surroundings and odors will go a long way toward establishing a feeling of ease and trust.

Unfortunately, the first encounter many veterinarians may have with a Rottweiler involves a snarling beast brought in by an owner who lacks control of the dog. Conversely, many Rottweilers have found themselves challenged by the veterinarian who fears the breed and attempts to establish dominance rather than rapport. If a veterinarian will not cooperate with you in making the experience a positive one for your Rottweiler, I suggest changing veterinarians.

YOUR PUPPY'S VACCINES

Vaccines are given to prevent your dog from getting an infectious disease like canine distemper or rabies. Vaccines are the ultimate preventive medicine: they're given before your dog ever gets the disease so as to protect him from the disease. That's why it is necessary for your dog to be vaccinated routinely. Puppy vaccines start at eight weeks of age for the five-in-one DHLPP vaccine and are given every three to four weeks until the puppy is sixteen months old. Your veterinarian will put your puppy on a proper schedule and will remind you when to bring in your dog for shots.

Vaccines: For What and When

Modern-day pet owners are fortunate in that their veterinarians can vaccinate their dogs against many infectious diseases that were almost always fatal. For the first few weeks of its life, your Rottweiler will enjoy the immunity provided by the antibodies present in the colostrum (first milk) from its mother. If the mother hasn't developed any immunity, neither will the puppy. The primary vaccinations required are those against *distemper, infectious hepatitis, parvovirus, leptospirosis, parainfluenza* and *coronavirus.*

In addition, most states require that dogs be vaccinated against rabies; the age may vary from state to state, but most veterinarians recommend the first dose be administered somewhere between three and four months of age. Usually, the first vaccination is good for one year. The next vaccination may be with a vaccine that is effective for three years; thereafter, it must be administered every three years.

Most veterinarians administer a "galaxy" dose; that is, one shot may contain several vaccines. Some puppies may experience a mild reaction to vaccines and be droopy for a few hours afterward; it's also not uncommon to observe some swelling and tenderness where the shot was administered. These are certainly minor inconveniences when you consider the alternative of not having the puppy immunized.

The Rottweiler is one of several breeds that sometimes experiences difficulty in building sufficient immunity against parvovirus, even though it has been vaccinated properly. To be certain that your Rottweiler has immunity, ask your veterinarian to pull blood and have the titer count (strength of immunity) tested. Your Rottweiler may require additional immunization. Generally, booster shots are administered yearly for this disease; however, in breeds that fail to build proper immunity or in those animals that are exposed to a variety of environments (owners who travel with their dogs, visit public parks, dog shows, etc.), more frequent boosters may be indicated. Avoid having private, unlicensed individuals give your dogs shots, no matter what.

Vaccines must be kept under carefully controlled conditions and administered by those who know what they're doing and are capable of reacting to a problem, for instance, anaphylactic shock. In addition, when a veterinarian administers the shots, you have the advantage of having the puppy inspected for problems you may not have noticed. Because there may be infectious dogs in the waiting room, puppies should always be carried in and kept on your lap; do not allow them to sniff the floor or touch noses with other animals.

Internal Parasites

Roundworms are the most common internal parasite to which the dog is subject. They live in the intestine and appear to be most prevalent in the juvenile animal (i.e., those under six months old). Puppies become infected with roundworms from the mother, not necessarily because she is infected but because pregnancy seems to activate dormant larvae, which migrate to the unborn puppies. Severely infected puppies may actually vomit worms and frequently pass them in their stool; the worms resemble strands of moving spaghetti. If untreated, roundworms can be fatal to puppies, although they seldom present a serious problem to the adult. Adults acquire roundworms through touching and ingesting soil containing the eggs. Only a few of the larvae will make it to the intestine; the rest will become encapsulated in tissue and remain dormant.

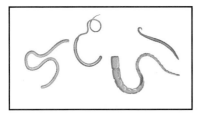

Common internal parasites (l-r): roundworm, whipworm, tapeworm and hookworm.

Tapeworms live in the small intestine; their heads fasten to the wall of the intestine, and their bodies may grow from one to several inches in length. Frequently, segments break off and are passed by the dog. These segments sometimes move; you may notice them in the dog's stool. If you notice small objects resembling white rice around the dog's anus, this is evidence of tapeworms. There is more than one kind of tapeworm, and more than one method of acquiring them. The most common carrier is the flea. Fleas acquire tapeworms by eating tapeworm eggs; the dog bites or swallows the flea, thus ingesting the immature tapeworm. Children can acquire a tapeworm the same way. One type of tapeworm is commonly found in cattle, sheep, horses, deer, elk and so forth; if raw meat from one of these infected animals is eaten, the dog will ingest the tapeworm eggs. The human may come in contact with the eggs in the dog's feces; although the eggs will not produce tapeworms in a human, they produce cysts in the liver, lungs and brain, which can result in a serious or even fatal illness. Some tapeworms are acquired by the dog's eating raw fresh fish, raw meat or game and carrion containing tapeworm eggs.

Hookworms are small, narrow worms sometimes acquired by touching contaminated feces or soil but most often by puppies' ingesting their mother's milk. Many animals that recover from an infestation of hookworms become carriers because of the larvae cysts carried in their tissue. Puppies with acute infestations require active veterinary attention.

Whipworms are about two inches long, slender and thickest at one end. In certain areas where the soil is heavily contaminated with eggs, infestations in dogs may be quite heavy. Usually, treatment has to be repeated over a considerable period.

Threadworms are representative of their name. Both eggs and larvae are passed in the feces. Some hazard to human health exists, mostly in tropical climates. Treatment must be repeated frequently; gaining control can be a lengthy process.

Good care on your part will help keep your Rottweiler healthy.

In most instances the presence of worms can be ascertained by submitting a fresh sample of the dog's stool to the veterinarian. In some cases, very sophisticated tests, of more than one type, must be performed. Owners who worm randomly with over-the-counter preparations are putting their dogs at risk. The determination of which worms are present is best left to your veterinarian, as is the choice and dosage of the deworming medication. Anything that kills worms can also kill the animal when administered incorrectly or if the animal is in a state of stress or debilitation.

In addition to the more common worms already named, there are at least three others worth mentioning here: **Pinworms** cause great concern to families with children and dogs. Despite the fact that dogs (and cats) are frequently blamed for pinworms found in humans, the animals are wrongly accused because they neither acquire nor spread human pinworms. **Flukes** are flat, come in more than one variety and are indigenous to several areas of the United States. To reduce the risk of infection, don't feed or let your dog eat raw fish, and restrict the animal from running free where aquatic snails, crayfish, infective vegetation or raw dead fish (particularly salmon, the cause of many canine deaths in the Pacific Northwest) might be found.

Heartworms are a threat to dogs almost anywhere in North America. Undetected and untreated, heartworms are eventually fatal. In severely infested dogs, treatment (which may include surgery) may be life-saving, but the dog frequently fails to regain its former vigor. Heartworm infection begins when an infective mosquito deposits its larvae in the skin. Six to seven months pass before the worm completes its cycle, and during this period it undergoes many transformations; eventually, the adult worm ends up in the right side of the heart. It is now sexually mature. If both sexes are present, they mate, and in a single day the female produces as many as five thousand live young, called *microfilaria*. These can remain alive and active in the bloodstream of the dog for up to three years. If the infected dog is bitten by a mosquito, that mosquito can then infect other animals.

Dogs that live in areas conducive to the breeding of the mosquito are thought to be most susceptible; however, since mosquitoes can be transported inadvertently by car, truck, train or plane, dogs everywhere are at risk. In the past, prevention involved the daily administration of arsenic. Arsenic has a cumulative propensity, and if the dog lived long enough, the preventive treatment itself might have proved fatal. Even today arsenic is part of the treatment of dogs infected with heartworms.

Some breeds (usually not Rottweilers) are sensitive to certain types of preventives, and these dogs may require specific medication daily, year-round, after first being tested to determine that no microfilaria are present in the bloodstream. Such medication kills the infective larvae before they mature into young adults and travel to the heart. If one dose is skipped, the chain of control is broken, and the dog is at risk. This was true of all heartworm medications until 1987, when the FDA approved Ivermectin. This drug is considered a true preventive rather than an after-the-fact treatment. It prevents larvae from developing into adults, even those that have infected the dog for as long as two months previously. As a result, dogs do not need to be heartworm-free before starting the medication.

Some veterinarians recommend abstinence from treatment during cold weather, when mosquitoes are dormant. If I lived in Alaska I might agree; however, there are few states in which live mosquitoes cannot be found in any month, and I prefer not to risk my dogs' lives. Once I start them on an Ivermectin treatment, my dogs stay on it during their entire lives. Puppies can be started as early as nine to twelve weeks of age. I usually start mine about four months, knowing they had immunity from their mother's milk for the first two months. Dosage is dependent on body weight, and the medication is given once a month, orally. It is available in pill form or tasty chewables.

At about six months of age, I upgrade puppies to a medication that prevents heartworm disease *and* treats and controls ascarid (roundworms) and hookworm infections in dogs. Heartworm medications can only be obtained through a veterinarian: an adult-dog dosage costs me about three dollars a month. Having witnessed the postmortem of a dog so badly infested that the heart actually split in two, I feel this is a small price to pay.

External Parasites

Fleas are not an inevitable adjunct to dog ownership. In some parts of the world the battle against this pest is constant; in other areas, a more casual attitude may be adopted, particularly if climate is your ally. Fleas do not live above an altitude of five thousand feet. The bottom line is never relax your vigilance against the flea and certain other external parasites. To fight the battle well, you must be informed of your enemy's vulnerabilities and never give an inch. Those who agree with the old saying that a dog needs a few fleas to keep him from being depressed about being a dog have already surrendered and lost the war.

The flea has two rapier-sharp devices for slitting open skin, saliva that keeps blood from clotting and an efficient strawlike projection that enables it to suck blood. Also, they are disc-shaped, flat, hard and have six legs, the rear pair of which would be the envy of any high- or broad-jumping competitor. If they were a few sizes larger, fleas would be the stuff of nightmares or mutant monster movies.

There are several hundred varieties of fleas, most having the same requirements (a warm-blooded host and a comfortable environment), and most following the same reproductive ritual, that is, an egg, larva, pupa and adult. The female can lay forty to fifty eggs a day, usually during the first four to nine days on the host. Most of the eggs fall to the floor or the dog's bedding. The larvae hatch within a few days, and their principal diet is the excrement of adult fleas (flea dirt), which is full of blood. Dogs that are seriously infested with fleas will have tiny cinder-like deposits, usually on their chests; this is flea dirt.

A couple of weeks after hatching, the larvae will spin a cocoon, which might transform into an adult flea in as short a span as a week or as long as a year. Fleas may

FIGHTING FLEAS

Remember, the fleas you see on your dog are only part of the problem—the smallest part! To rid your dog and home of fleas, you need to treat your dog *and* your home. Here's how:

• Identify where your pet(s) sleep. These are "hot spots."

• Clean your pets' bedding regularly by vacuuming and washing.

• Spray "hot spots" with a nontoxic, long-lasting flea larvicide.

• Treat outdoor "hot spots" with insecticide.

• Kill eggs on pets with a product containing insect growth regulators (IGRs).

• Kill fleas on pets per your veterinarian's recommendation.

live as long as three years! Many dogs are highly allergic to the saliva of the flea, and this reaction will cause them much more aggravation than the actual bite. Dogs so afflicted need prompt and regular attention from their veterinarian. It is inaccurate to think of the flea as only a minor nuisance. It's a filthy parasite (the dog flea is an intermediate host for tapeworms, and the rodent flea carries bubonic plague), but you can gain the upper hand without destroying the environment with radical insecticides. No matter how careful you may be, there are causes of flea infestation over which you have no control.

These specks in your dog's fur mean he has fleas.

Dogs usually acquire fleas from other dogs or cats. If flea-carrying cats, rats, possums or squirrels trespass across your yard, they may shed flea eggs, which become larva, which become adult fleas, which hop on your dog, that becomes their mobile smorgasbord as well as their meal ticket into your house and yard.

The first line of defense against fleas is cleanliness. Flea larvae are usually found at the base of carpet fibers and are resistant even to vacuum cleaning. Regular vacuuming will, however, remove their food source, adult flea feces. Throw rugs and dog bedding must be laundered weekly with extremely hot water. Any place your dog is apt to spend a few minutes (furniture, the car, etc.) will require regular vacuuming and cleaning. If your dog has picked up adult fleas, the best remedy is to immediately use an insecticide spray or shampoo. I use a product whose primary ingredient is pyrethrin (a synthetic compound modeled after that found in chrysanthemums), and it will kill the adult flea.

Controlling Fleas

The only way to control fleas is to break their reproductive cycle. Although you may have removed the adult fleas from the dog, chances are eggs have been laid on the premises. Products are available that are both easy to use and safe. One is a spray that contains methoprene, a flea growth inhibitor that doesn't kill anything; it prevents flea larvae and pupae from developing into adult fleas. They remain juveniles and eventually die without ever having reproduced. There is also a spray for outdoor areas that contains a beneficial nematode, a tiny organism that eats the larvae of harmful insects. Because a nematode eats only pests, it is called a biopesticide. It enters the flea through body openings, then releases bacteria lethal to the flea. The nematodes feed on the flea's body, reproduce and search for more fleas. Once all the fleas are gone, the nematodes die and decompose. This product is safe for mammals, beneficial insects and plants. Because it's not a chemical, no buildup of resistance occurs. It's only disadvantage is that it's expensive to apply to a large area.

Relying on flea powder, flea collars or medallions and home remedies will not bring you freedom from fleas. Flea powder must be applied often; the insecticide dust can get into your lungs as well as the dog's. Flea

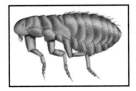

The flea is a die-hard pest.

collars or medallions (very popular because the concept pleases dog owners—they don't have to lift a finger) are not very effective. Some hazard exists, especially to young puppies, from absorption, inhalation or ingestion of the toxin. Care must be taken not to worm dogs with the same toxin used in the collar because the combined dose could prove fatal. Home remedies (garlic, brewer's yeast, sulphur, etc.) might affect the number of fleas on a dog but will have no impact on flea larvae or eggs.

Systemic insecticides, neurotoxic to fleas, are available only through a veterinarian. The dose is administered orally and will be present in the dog's bloodstream. The flea must feed on the dog several times before it accumulates enough insecticide to die. During this period, the female flea could lay many eggs. It is not recommended for pregnant or nursing bitches and has other restrictions as well, including being highly toxic to humans and the dog. I, personally, would rather try other methods than introduce toxins into my dog.

Ticks are pests that don't do much damage with their bite but may transmit serious diseases to dogs, livestock and humans. As with fleas, their anticoagulating saliva causes a severe reaction in some dogs. Again, the ounce of prevention is worth a pound of cure. These tiny arachnids are not only repulsive, especially when full of blood, but also are extremely dangerous to the touch, even without biting. Ticks are most prevalent in the spring and summer; careful examination, using fingers as well as eyes and paying particular attention to ears, neck, throat, head and between the toes each time the dog returns from being outdoors, can prevent your dog from becoming a feeding and breeding ground for ticks.

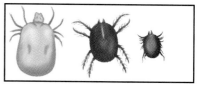

Several species of ticks live on the dog. The engorged tick (easily noticed because of its size, almost as big as a pea) is the female; if you look closely, you'll usually find the much smaller male nearby. All species of the tick can transmit diseases, which include Rocky Mountain spotted fever, tularemia, canine ehrlichiosis (thought to have been introduced to this country by dogs of the military returning from service in Vietnam; many forms of ehrlichiosis exist) and several others. Ehrlichiosis is primarily a problem in the southern states because the brown dog tick, its vector, continues activity even during colder months. Some ticks secrete a toxin that causes paralysis in dogs.

Three types of ticks (l-r): the wood tick, brown dog tick and deer tick.

Lyme Disease

Probably the most feared disease from ticks is Lyme disease, first identified in 1975 in Lyme, Connecticut. Both animals and humans can contract this malady, frightening not because of its mortality rate but because of its uncertain and frequently incorrect diagnosis, its debilitating and persistent symptoms and its erratically successful and usually prolonged treatment. Prevention is made difficult by the fact that the transmitting tick is usually in the nymphal stage of development and is about the size of a comma. Victims are seldom aware that the tick is feeding unless they observe a "freckle" move.

If you find a tick imbedded in your Rottweiler's body, do *not* attempt to remove it with bare fingers because the blood of ticks can carry diseases dangerous to

people. Apply some alcohol, gin, ether or insecticide to the tick with a cotton-tipped applicator. The tick will be dead in a few moments. Using tweezers, grasp the tick as close to the skin as possible, and pull steadily to dislodge. If the head remains imbedded, it will fester and come out in a few days. Ticks should be disposed of by burning or drowning. It's almost impossible to kill one by stepping on it. If ticks are deep within the ear of the dog, the animal must be anesthetized and the ticks removed with forceps. It is a job for your veterinarian.

Use tweezers to remove ticks from your dog.

Many dips are efficacious in discouraging ticks from climbing on your dog, and your veterinarian can recommend one. Most flea collars are also advertised as discouraging ticks, but in neither case are they very efficient, and they have many disadvantages. My choice, for the four months of the year that ticks are really active in my area (Pacific Northwest—May, June, July, August) is a collar available through veterinarians. It is adjustable and should be placed loosely around the dog's neck. It should be removed for prolonged swimming and other contact with water and then replaced. Local houndsmen, whose dogs spend much more time in the woods and fields than mine do, have used it for several years with remarkable results.

Lice are not ordinarily found in healthy, well-maintained dogs. There are two types: one that bites and feeds on skin scales, and one that sucks blood. The latter can cause anemia. If lice are found, the dog's bedding must be destroyed and its sleeping quarters disinfected.

Mites are a different kettle of fish. They are common as dirt and come in almost as many varieties. The ones you are most apt to have to deal with are listed below. Ear mites are tiny bugs that live in ear canals and feed on skin debris. They are the most common cause of ear infections in puppies and young dogs; if both ears are affected, suspect ear mites. Symptoms include violent head shaking and ear scratching. Confirm your suspicion by removing some earwax with a cotton-tipped applicator and observing it under a microscope against a dark background. Mites will be the white specks, pinhead size, that move. At times the mites will migrate from the ear canals and travel over the body. They are highly contagious to both dogs and cats. Other pets in the household will have to be treated.

Once ear mites have been identified, treat with a miticide twice weekly for three full weeks. If you stop treatment too soon, a new crop of mites will reinfest the dog because the medication does not destroy eggs. An insecticide dip or spray will have to be used on the body to kill the traveling mites. Frequently, the ear problem is compounded by bacterial infection. Medications are available that contain a miticide (to kill the mites), an antibiotic (to treat the bacterial infection) and a steroid (to reduce the itching).

Mange

Sarcoptic mange (scabies) is also caused by a mite. In terms of severe discomfort, nothing can equal the scratching and biting caused by this mite. The female tunnels under the skin to lay her eggs, which hatch in three to ten days. The newly hatched mites develop into adults and start to lay their eggs under the skin, the whole process requiring seventeen to twenty-one days. These mites prefer the skin of the ears, elbows, hocks and face. Symptoms are hair loss, crusty skin, and red, itchy bumps. In the final stages skin becomes thick and darkly pigmented, and serum may ooze from skin breaks. If your Rottweiler is infested, you may notice itching of your skin at the beltline—the mites have transferred to you. However, they will not live over three weeks on human skin. The dog will require veterinary assistance because insecticide dips (at least three with intervals of ten days in between) are indicated as well as is cortisone to relieve the itching. Infected sores from scratching or biting may need to be treated with an antibiotic.

Cheyletiella mange (walking dandruff) commonly attacks puppies, is highly contagious and usually infests kennels. Control can be had by following the same procedure as used for scabies.

Demodectic mange, although common, is not fully understood. Most dogs acquire the mange mites early in life from their mothers and don't have a problem. It has been ventured that stress may cause an outbreak of demodectic mange, especially if that stress occurs during puberty when sebum (what the mite feeds on) increases in the dog. Localized demodectic mange occurs in dogs up to age one, starting as a thinning of the hair around the eyes and on the face, which causes an almost mask-like appearance. If more than five patches of affected area are present, chances are the disease is escalating to the generalized form. Treatment involves medicated dips (usually Mitaban) as well as antibiotics. Cortisone is contraindicated because it may suppress the natural immunity of the dog, worsening the condition. Early diagnosis and treatment is essential, but demodectic mange is very serious, and a veterinarian may not always be able to effect a cure.

WHEN TO CALL THE VET

In any emergency situation, you should call your veterinarian immediately. You can make the difference in your dog's life by staying as calm as possible when you call and by giving the doctor or the assistant as much information as possible before you leave for the clinic. That way, the vet will be able to take immediate, specific action to remedy your dog's situation.

Emergencies include acute abdominal pain, suspected poisoning, snakebite, burns, frostbite, shock, dehydration, abnormal vomiting or bleeding, and deep wounds. You are the best judge of your dog's health, as you live with and observe him every day. Don't hesitate to call your veterinarian if you suspect trouble.

Skin Problems

Except for nose and footpads, your Rottweiler's skin is thinner and more susceptible to damage than is yours; unlike yours, it contains no sweat glands except in the footpads. Careless use of grooming tools can cause damage to the skin. Once the skin is broken, by whatever method, the condition tends to spread.

Skin problems are difficult to diagnose and even more difficult to treat. They are broken down into five major headings:

1. Itchy skin disorders (which include all the external parasites previously mentioned as well as lick sores and food allergy dermatitis);

2. Poor hair growth or hair loss: A-type—(hormone-related) and B-type—(other than hormone-related);

3. Painful skin disorders with pus drainage (pyoderma);

4. Autoimmune skin diseases;

5. Lumps or bumps (on or beneath the skin). This category includes everything from the tender lump frequently found at a vaccination site to a cancerous tumor. Many times the lump is of no significance. However, certain indications may warn of serious trouble—for instance, rapid growth; appearing hard and fixed to surrounding tissue; growing from bone; bleeding; a mole that spreads or ulcerates; an unexplained open sore, resistant to healing; any lump in the breast. A biopsy is indicated if any of these conditions exists and is the only means of certain diagnosis.

An Elizabethan collar keeps your dog from licking a fresh wound.

Rottweilers seem to have a genetic predisposition to cancer, and owners would be well advised to be very alert to early warning signs, and consult with a veterinarian as soon as the symptom is noted.

Eye Problems

Your Rottweiler will tell you in no uncertain manner if it is having an eye problem. Symptoms include pus in the eye, watering eye, squinting and pawing at the eye. Many times an examination in good light will reveal the culprit, usually a grass seed or something similar. Frequently, the object can be removed by a cotton-tipped applicator that has first been moistened. Often, the foreign body will stick to it. Irrigation of the eye can be effected by saturating a wad of cotton with a saltwater solution (one teaspoonful salt to one pint water) and squeezing the liquid into the eye, following up by applying an ophthalmic ointment.

Squeeze eye ointment into the lower lid.

Application of ointments is easily achieved by pulling down the lower eyelid and applying the ointment to the inner surface of the eyelid. If you attempt to apply it directly to the eyeball, the dog will resist, and you might damage the eyeball. Eyedrops may be applied directly to the eyeball. Never use a product that is not specifically labeled for ophthalmic use. If the product is out of date or no date is apparent, do not use it. If an object has penetrated the eyeball, immediate veterinary care should be sought. All too often the object is hidden behind the third eyelid (your dog has one, you don't), a membrane that acts almost like a windshield wiper, cleansing and lubricating as it sweeps across the eye. If this is the case, the dog must usually be anesthetized before proper examination can be performed and the offending object removed.

One of the most common eye disorders in Rottweilers, in addition to foreign bodies, is *Entropion*—where the eyelid rolls inward (usually the lower eyelid), a condition now quite common in the Rottweiler and correctable only by surgery. The condition is quite distressing to the dog (see Chapter 1). Another common disorder is *Progressive Retinal Atrophy* (PRA)—this condition is characterized by degeneration of the cells of the retina, leading eventually to blindness. It is caused by a simple recessive trait, and, for this reason, ethical breeders have their prospective breeding stock examined and certified free of this disorder by the Canine Eye Registration Foundation (established in 1974).

Other disorders such as glaucoma or cataracts may have to be dealt with by the Rottweiler owner. However, these disorders are not generally breed specific. Because the eye is such a complex mechanism, many general practice veterinarians prefer to refer patients to an eye specialist for extraordinary problems.

Your Rottweiler's Nose

The dog's nose contains far more nerve endings than does the nose of a human. They connect with a highly developed olfactory center in the brain and have a scenting ability at least one hundred times superior to that of humans, although no one can explain how it actually functions or what it is the dog actually smells— disturbed vegetation, disturbed air, body scents and so forth. The nose has no sweat glands, although it's normally cool and moist, the moisture coming from mucus glands in the lining. It is not always true that a warm, dry nose is indicative of a fever or that a cool nose indicates lack of same. Although dogs seldom have nosebleeds, the nose is an extremely sensitive organ, and much damage can be done by poking objects in it. Some dogs, when they become very excited, may secrete a clear, watery fluid that disappears when the dog is again calm. It's nothing you should be concerned about.

Dogs don't catch colds as humans do—if the dog has a runny nose, mucus in the eyes, accompanied by a cough or fever, get it to a veterinarian. Chances are some viral disease (such as distemper) is at work, and the dog is at risk. Frenzied sneezing, accompanied by frantic pawing at the nose, usually indicates a foreign body. The dog needs to be examined by a veterinarian.

Although the breed standard of the Rottweiler calls for a black nose (see Chapter 1), it's not uncommon to observe a lack of pigmentation. In the case of vitiligo, a gradual loss of pigmentation may occur until the nose, and sometimes the lips, are a chocolate brown. Sometimes, the dog regains its former dark pigmentation without interference. There is another condition called "snow nose" or "winter nose" in which the black pigment lightens during the winter, then darkens in summer. Thought by many to afflict primarily white-coated breeds, it is suspected that a hereditary predisposition exists in some bloodlines. It is a cosmetic condition, not rare in Rottweilers. Some dogs are sensitive to the agents found in plastic or rubber dishes and may develop inflamed noses with loss of pigmentation. One of the most common problems is a foreign object in the nose. Unless the object can be grasped from outside the nose, a trip to the veterinarian is called for.

Run your hands regularly over your dog to feel for any injuries.

Foxtails

Of all the things on this earth that plague man and dog, in my estimation, the foxtail is probably the worst because where I live, they are a curse. Every spring from about mid-May to the end of July the foxtail, a barbed awn with a sharp point, prevents me from walking and running my dogs. Usually found in wheat-growing areas, this pest is very lightweight, easily inhaled by the dog into its nose or lodged in its ear or eye. It's barbed enough to cling to rear or belly hair, from where it then makes its way into the anus, vagina or penile sheath. That in itself is bad enough, but this terrible object keeps moving forward under the skin, through vessels and so forth. It has been known to travel to the heart and kill the dog. The only means of prevention is to keep the dog away from open fields.

When traveling in areas where the foxtail is prevalent, I will use a vegetable oil, creme rinse or similar product on my dog's feet, around the anus, ears, eyes, nose, lips and chest. The foxtail cannot stick to such a slippery surface, and though it may cling to the hairs, it cannot travel and is easily removed.

Caring for the Ears

Your Rottweiler seldom needs to have its ears cleaned, a certain amount of earwax being needed to maintain health of the tissue. If the ear appears to need cleaning, moisten a soft cloth with some mineral oil, wrap it around your finger and use your finger as a swab. A cotton swab can be used. Remember that the ear canal drops vertically before it makes a sharp turn to continue as the horizontal ear canal, ending at the eardrum. Don't poke long sharp objects into the ear; nor should you introduce any kind of liquid (including water) or solvent into the dog's ear by any method.

Dirty ears should be closely monitored as they may indicate trouble. Foreign objects can cause serious problems and the pesky foxtail is one of the more common causes of ear infections. If your Rottweiler is sent to a professional groomer, instruct him not to pull the hair from beneath the ear flap. This breed does not grow sufficient hair in that area to interfere with air circulation, and pulling the hair out causes serum to ooze from the pores, opening the door to infection. It is not a necessary procedure in the Rottweiler.

A healthy dog is full of life and energy.

Early on, your Rottweiler puppy should be taught to patiently submit to an examination of its mouth, not a perfunctory one such as a conformation judge might do, but a thorough examination to pinpoint any problems. Trouble spots to look for are sore-looking, inflamed gums; teeth with a buildup of tartar; and bad breath. Periodontal disease is as much a problem for some dogs as it is for some people, and so is gingivitis. Mouth problems you may be less familiar with include strangulation of the tongue—a sudden swelling usually caused by a rubber band or piece of thread or string becoming wrapped around the tongue. The struggles of the dog to dislodge it only move it farther back on the tongue until locating the offending object becomes very difficult. Dogs that occupy themselves with removing small burrs, splinters and so forth from their feet frequently will cause their tongues to become sore. Often, an object will be removed from the dog's feet by penetration of the tongue. Inspect the tongue closely, and if it is penetrated by foreign objects, remove them carefully with tweezers.

Taking Care of Teeth

Proper care of the teeth does much to protect your Rottweiler's overall health. Teeth should be cleaned regularly. Use a rough cloth, moistened, to scrub the teeth vigorously. Brush teeth and gums twice a week

Check your dog's teeth frequently and brush them regularly.

with a toothpaste for dogs, not for people. Feed a hard biscuit once daily and something hard to chew on once or twice a week. Chewing of rubber and tennis balls has no beneficial result as far as dental care goes. Generally, despite your best efforts, there may come a time when the teeth need to be professionally cleaned. This is not as simple as it sounds. The dog doesn't like it any better than you do and is not prepared to submit to this unpleasant procedure. Anesthesia must be administered to accomplish the task.

Most owners of large, deep-chested dogs are well aware of the hazards of anesthesia and frequently drag their heels, trying to decide if the result justifies the risk. My belief is that it does, and I substantiate it by the fact that I often undergo general anesthesia for certain dental procedures for which I don't care to be present. I would not use a veterinarian in whom I had such little faith that I questioned his or her ability to safely administer anesthesia. Second, I'm well aware of the serious complications that can develop because of poor dental hygiene and opt for the lesser of the two evils. I clean my dogs' teeth regularly but usually end up having them scaled by my veterinarian about every one to two years, depending on their age.

Spaying and Neutering

Spaying or neutering will relieve your Rottweiler of certain characteristics that might interfere with the dog's ability to be an enjoyable companion and will also depress certain instincts that are not pleasant to live with. More important, the procedures completely prevent puppies from being brought into a world that cannot deal with the dogs it already has. Of equal importance to most owners is the fact that a bitch, subsequent to an ovariohysterectomy (removal of uterus, tubes and ovaries), *cannot* get uterine cancer or ovarian cancer, and her chances of getting mammary cancer are greatly reduced. After a bitch is spayed, the owner can say good-bye to the risk of pyometra as well as the mess and inconvenience of two heat cycles a year.

Males also receive benefits from being neutered. Danger from testicular cancer is gone. Many males suffer from one undescended testicle, a condition that frequently creates a problem. Some testicular tumors secrete estrogen and cause feminization of the male, a condition remedied once the testicles are removed. Castration of the male for the sole purpose of improving the dog's attitude seldom produces the desired results. If the male is obnoxious and aggressive, urinates deliberately in the house and so on, he is in dire need of training. Castration may tone down the temperament of a male if performed at an early age.

Until recently, the standard time for spaying or neutering was after the bitch was six months old and before her first heat cycle. Many think neutering a male before puberty can seriously affect his bone development, stature and secondary sex traits. Much research over recent years has led the American Veterinary Medical Association and the AKC to go on public record in 1993 as advocating and supporting early (eight to sixteen weeks) spaying and neutering.

Some people believe (1) spaying or neutering will cause the dog to become fat and lazy. *Not true!* Overfeeding and inadequate exercise cause a dog to become fat and lazy. (2) Spaying or neutering will cause the dog to be a "sissy." *Not true!* Temperament genes are locked in at conception and will be affected only by environment. (3) An unneutered male must be occasionally bred to give the dog some "relief." *Not true!* Unlike people, dogs are not excited by pictures and similar external stimuli. (4) A female craves motherhood. *Not true!* Her emotional needs are met by human companionship.

ADVANTAGES OF SPAY/NEUTER

The greatest advantage of spaying (for females) or neutering (for males) your dog is that you are guaranteed your dog will not produce puppies. There are too many puppies already available for too few homes. There are other advantages as well.

ADVANTAGES OF SPAYING

No messy heats.

No "suitors" howling at your windows or waiting in your yard.

Decreased incidences of pyometra (disease of the uterus) and breast cancer.

ADVANTAGES OF NEUTERING

Lessens male aggressive and territorial behaviors, but doesn't affect the dog's personality. Behaviors are often owner-induced, so neutering is not the only answer, but it is a good start.

Prevents the need to roam in search of bitches in season.

Decreased incidences of urogenital diseases.

The Intact Bitch

If you have a female Rottweiler and decide to keep her intact (unspayed), you should be aware of certain difficulties. Your Rottweiler will probably come in heat twice a year, although some bitches come in every four months, and certain breeds come in once a year. If you don't want her to breed, you must keep her in the house and allow her out only on leash in custody of an adult. The estrous cycle will last at least three weeks; most of that time a house dog will have to wear "bitches britches" or some form of sanitary napkin.

The first portion of the cycle consists of a dark, bloody discharge, accompanied by firm swelling of the vulva. The odor in her urine starts to attract males; the bitch will not be receptive at this time and may sit down if a male attempts to mount or may even growl and snap at a persistent suitor. This period lasts six to nine days; then begins the estrus or standing heat. The discharge fades to a watery pink and the vulva softens. Now the female will be very receptive. She will be coy and flirtatious with a male, lift her pelvis and present her vulva when touched in the rear. This behavior usually starts about two days before she ovulates. The third phase is unremarkable as far as pet ownership is concerned. The female will no longer stand for the male, the discharge ceases and the male loses interest. Breasts and vulva will remain somewhat larger than before. *Do not be caught off guard!* Many bitches will opt for a last-minute fling.

About six to ten weeks after the heat period, even though not bred, the female may show every sign of being pregnant, including milk in the breasts. The bitch may want to make a nest and start to mother inanimate objects. She can become quite paranoid. Many years ago I had a bitch who decided that a large, red ball was the perfect puppy substitute. It even had a "navel," a slight depression where the seam was, and she would lick this endlessly, keeping her "baby" clean. A dear friend was with me at a dog show where I had this bitch, her "puppy" being carried gently in her mouth. We were having a conversation with a group about false pregnancies. "How long do they keep this up?" someone asked. "As long as you let them," my friend responded, removing the ball from

IDENTIFYING YOUR DOG

It's a terrible thing to think about, but your dog could somehow, someday, get lost or stolen. How would you get him back? Your best bet would be to have some form of identification on your dog. You can choose from a collar and tags, a tattoo, a microchip or a combination of these three.

Every dog should wear a buckle collar with identification tags. They are the quickest and easiest way for a stranger to identify your dog. It's best to inscribe the tags with your name and phone number; you don't need to include your dog's name.

There are two ways to permanently identify your dog. The first is a tattoo, placed on the inside of your dog's thigh. The tattoo should be your social security number or your dog's AKC registration number.

The second is a microchip, a rice-sized pellet that's inserted under the dog's skin at the base of the neck, between the shoulder blades. When a scanner is passed over the dog, it will beep, notifying the person that the dog has a chip. The scanner will then show a code, identifying the dog. Microchips are becoming more and more popular and are certainly the wave of the future.

the dog's mouth and dropping it into her purse. The poor dog never saw her "baby" again and within ten minutes had forgotten all about it.

Spaying is the best cure for false pregnancies. The male can detect the scent of a flowering bitch from an extreme distance. He will become restless and attempt to escape from enclosures. Once he reaches the object of his desire, he will hang around with great anticipation, frequently oblivious to other males in competition. If your household contains an intact male and intact female, regardless of breed or relationship, anticipate difficulties. For the three weeks of the bitches' estrous cycle, some males may refuse to eat; some howl their frustrations; others completely lose their wits and have only one thing on their minds; many have been known to gnaw through doors and chain-link fences to reach the female.

An old saying goes, "If you don't want your female to have puppies, when she starts to come in heat, board up the doors, windows and chimney and keep her inside for three weeks. In 63 days expect puppies." Males and females are both very determined to obey nature's call to reproduce. The only sure method of birth control is to spay and neuter.

Urogenital Problems

In almost all mature male canines, a small amount of yellowish discharge is present at the opening of the sheath. Treatment with antibiotics may temporarily clear up the discharge, but when the treatment is over, the discharge will reappear. It's normal and not cause for concern. However, if the dog begins to lick himself excessively and has a foul-smelling discharge, the symptoms indicate an infection. Grass awns and other debris may lodge under the foreskin and cause infection. Treatment consists of clipping away the hair near the foreskin and pushing back the foreskin to expose the penis head. Wash the area thoroughly with a surgical soap and apply an antibiotic ointment. If the dog is not willing to have the foreskin retracted, fill a syringe with diluted hydrogen peroxide solution, and flush twice daily. Follow up by infusing the sheath with antibiotic ointment.

In the female, bacterial infection of the vagina is not uncommon, usually accompanied by painful urination. Frequently, it goes unnoticed because many bitches are fanatic about keeping that area clean. If there is a male around, however, he is misled into thinking she is in heat and reacts accordingly. If the bitch has already been spayed, you can be almost certain that this behavior indicates a vaginal infection. This is another infection often caused by that damnable thing, the foxtail. Bitches who squat close to the ground to urinate frequently pick up foxtails in the vagina. Locating them calls for great persistence by the veterinarian.

It's not uncommon for very young puppies (six to twelve weeks) to experience juvenile vaginitis. Douches and estrogen are usually prescribed.

Diagnosing Your Rottweiler

There are some things you can learn to do that will enable your veterinarian to more quickly arrive at a diagnosis and start treatment for whatever ails your pet.

Taking Your Dog's Temperature You should know how to take your dog's temperature. You can't feel the dog's brow, nose or any other part to determine if it's running a fever. The temperature must be taken rectally. Shake down the thermometer until the bulb registers 96 degrees Fahrenheit. Lubricate the bulb with petroleum jelly, raise the dog's tail and hold it firmly to keep the dog from sitting. Gently insert the bulb into the anal canal with a twisting motion, about two or two and a half inches for a Rottweiler. Hold it in place for three minutes, remove, wipe clean and read the temperature. Normal temperature for an adult dog is 100 degrees Fahrenheit to 102.5 degrees Fahrenheit. Clean the thermometer with alcohol before reusing. *Warning: If the dog sits down and breaks the thermometer, do not attempt to find and extract the broken end. Give one or* *two teaspoonsful of mineral oil orally to facilitate passage and notify your veterinarian.*

Despite the brevity of their tails, Rottweilers have extremely powerful muscles to control them. Grasping a Rottweiler's tail and holding it to one side can be very tricky. Frequently, taking the temperature will require an assistant.

Taking Your Dog's Pulse You should also know how to take your dog's pulse. It can be done with the dog standing or lying down. Feel on the inside of the thigh where leg and body join. Press until you feel the pulsation. The pulse rate, which is the same as the heart rate, should be 60 to 160 beats per minute. It may be somewhat slower in a large dog and faster in a puppy. It should be strong, steady and regular. Any deviation should be noted by you and described to your veterinarian. A pulse may also be taken by pressing against the rib cage over the heart. With the dog standing, feel the chest pulse just below the elbow joint.

If you're checking temperature and pulse to relay the information to your veterinarian, you should also check circulation. Gums or inner eyelids should be deep pink with good circulation. Quality of the circulation can be determined by checking the time it takes for the tissue to regain normal pink after the gum has been pressed firmly with a finger. If recovery occurs in one second or less, circulation is normal; a delay of two seconds suggests poor circulation; if three seconds or longer, the dog is in shock. A gray or bluish tinge to mucus membranes of lips and tongue is a sign of insufficient oxygen in the blood and may indicate heart and lung failure.

Diarrhea

Common problems afflicting the dog (in addition to those already mentioned) include diarrhea, which is a symptom, not a disease. Diarrhea is most frequently generated by something the dog has eaten, ranging from poor-quality food to disgusting garbage, from rocks to impure water. For simple diarrhea, treatment is basic—withhold all food and water for twenty-four to forty-eight hours. If still thirsty, give the dog ice cubes to lick or very small amounts of water. Drinking copious amounts of water can aggravate and prolong the diarrhea. Give Lomotil (one tablet per twenty-five pounds of body weight) three times per day. If improvement is noted, start feeding the dog cooked rice; lean chicken, turkey or lamb may be added (this diet is the most digestible for the dog), provided no fat is included. Soft-cooked eggs may also prove digestible. Continue this diet for three days before returning to normal feeding.

If diarrhea is accompanied by bloody stool, vomiting or fever or persists more than twenty-four hours, consult your veterinarian. Diarrhea is extremely debilitating and the cycle must be interrupted as quickly as possible.

Watch What Your Dog Drinks . . .

Many people believe a dog's tongue somehow magically "purifies" everything it drinks and that dogs can drink from standing puddles, stagnant pools and so forth with impunity. Nothing could be further from the truth. In addition to all the harmful bacteria such liquid contains, in today's world this water may also have a lethal dose of antifreeze and other unimaginable toxic pollutants. Do not permit your dog to drink from these places. When traveling, take along a sufficient supply of water from home. If you run out, it's safer to buy bottled water than to rely on unproven sources.

A FIRST-AID KIT

Keep a canine first-aid kit on hand for general care and emergencies. Check it periodically to make sure liquids haven't spilled or dried up, and replace medications and materials after they're used. Your kit should include:

Activated charcoal tablets

Adhesive tape
(1 and 2 inches wide)

Antibacterial ointment
(for skin and eyes)

Aspirin (buffered or enteric coated, not Ibuprofen)

Bandages: Gauze rolls (1 and 2 inches wide) and dressing pads

Cotton balls

Diarrhea medicine

Dosing syringe

Hydrogen peroxide (3%)

Petroleum jelly

Rectal thermometer

Rubber gloves

Rubbing alcohol

Scissors

Tourniquet

Towel

Tweezers

. . . and Eats

Botulism (*clostridium botulinum*) can be as much a problem for the dog as it is for the human. Particularly at risk are those dogs that have access to spoiled carcasses. The feces of waterfowl act as a carrier for the bacteria, and areas where waterfowl feed and rest in great numbers may prove hazardous. Bloat (gastric dilatation), also known as the overfeeding or overeating syndrome, simply means an extreme swelling of the stomach from gas, fluid or both.

Bloat and Volvulus

Bloat usually affects large, deep-chested dogs; affected animals are usually between four and seven years of age; two-thirds are males. Symptoms are excessive salivation, restlessness and attempts to vomit and defecate. The dog shows reaction to pain when you press on the stomach. The quickest way to provide relief as well as to determine that it is gastric dilatation and not the more serious torsion (where the stomach twists 180 degrees on its own axis; volvulus is when the stomach rotates more than 180 degrees) is to insert a long rubber hose into the stomach; as the tube enters the stomach, there is a rush of air, bringing immediate relief. In order to pass a stomach tube, first measure a length of tubing from the tip of the dog's nose to the last rib, then mark the tubing. Insert it behind one of the canine teeth and advance it into the throat until the dog begins to swallow. If the dog gags, continue to advance the tube. If the dog coughs, withdraw the tube and try again. There is small danger of damaging the esophagus with a soft rubber or plastic tube.

If the stomach has actually rotated, the tube cannot pass into it, and your dog is in extreme danger. You have about forty-five minutes to get the dog to a veterinarian with any hope of saving it. The torsion must be surgically corrected. New techniques in recent years have led many veterinarians to "tack" the stomach to the ribs to prevent future torsions.

Skeletal Concerns

The knee (called stifle joint in dogs) has two major bones and two cruciate ligaments, forming an X, which hold the bones in place. Repetitive traumatic impact on the stifle (such as fence running) or sudden twisting of the stifle while in flexion (such as when a running animal steps into a hole) can rupture the cruciate ligament. Surgical repair is required. Many breeds are particularly susceptible to certain disorders, and certain bloodlines within a breed may be "carriers" or more vulnerable than others. We have already spoken in this chapter of the predisposition of the Rottweiler to cancer, in many forms.

Your Rottweiler's Heart

In recent years there has been an alarming increase of heart problems within the breed; dilated cardiomyopathy (literally, disease of the heart muscle) is no longer a rarity. Subaortic stenosis is a killer of large breeds (*stenosis* meaning a "narrowing or constriction"); picture a kink in a garden hose, so a subaortic stenosis restricts the flow of blood from the heart to the brain and body. When more oxygen is required by the dog, due to exercise or excitement, it does not receive the oxygen and may suddenly collapse and die.

Use a scarf or old hose to make a temporary muzzle, as shown.

First Aid

Everyone should have a complete first-aid kit, both at home and in the car. Pet owners should make up a separate kit for their Rottweilers. It should include hydrogen peroxide, Mylanta, Lomotil, ophthalmic ointment, antibiotic ointment, mineral oil, syrup of ipecac, cotton, thermometer, tweezers, activated charcoal (not the stuff you barbecue with), gauze and adhesive tape. Keep extra sheets or blankets in the car. Most veterinarians would be happy to recommend items for a first-aid kit; many will also supply a first-aid pamphlet.

Skunks

There are as many recipes for removing skunk odor as there are for meatloaf. Some work, some don't. My personal favorite is a lovely product called Skunk-off. It really does remove, not mask, the odor, permanently.

Some of the many household substances harmful to your dog.

Stings

Stings from insects are sometimes quite painful, and if stung many times, a Rottweiler could go into shock

from the toxins. Always try to identify the insect (bee, wasp, spider); if a bee has left its stinger in the dog, remove it with tweezers. Many commercial preparations are available to treat insect stings, and one of these should be in your first-aid kit. If nothing else is available, make a paste of baking soda and water, and apply it directly to the site of the sting.

Poisoning

Poisoning needs to be treated by your veterinarian; it will be helpful to him if you can identify the poison. Take a good look at things around your house to make certain the dog has not ingested anything toxic.

Choking

Choking is indicated by forceful coughing, bulging eyes and frantic pawing at the mouth. It is necessary to open the dog's mouth and try to remove whatever is blocking the passageway. This is not always easy with a large strong dog, particularly if you're alone.

If you cannot see the object, lay the dog on its side with lowered head and elevated hindquarters; place both hands just beneath the rib cage and press in and up.

Continue pressing until the dog coughs up the object or becomes unconscious. Veterinary assistance must be sought at this point. If you have help, one person should drive and the other tend the dog. Place the dog on its side, head lowered, rear elevated, as before. Keep the airway open and the tongue pulled to one side. Place both hands just beneath the rib cage and press in and up, twice; check mouth for foreign bodies. Give two breaths (muzzle held closed, your mouth encompassing the dog's nose). Repeat until the dog is breathing on its own. Every few minutes, check for a pulse.

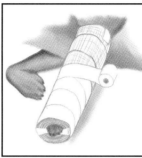

Make a temporary splint by wrapping the leg in firm casing, then bandaging it.

Giving Pills and Liquids

To administer a pill or tablet, stand to the side of the dog. Open the mouth by inserting an index finger behind the canine tooth on the upper jaw on the side away from you. Aren't you glad you taught your dog to do this as a puppy? It makes the procedure so much easier. Place the pill or tablet in the center of the tongue, to the rear. If you place it off-center, the dog will cleverly roll it forward and spit it out. Close the dog's mouth and gently hold it closed, stroking the throat until the dog swallows. If the dog licks its nose, the pill has probably been swallowed. Some pills that are very large or very dry may be slightly coated with butter to help swallowing (which also makes them more slippery for you to grasp).

Syringes and eyedroppers are great for administering liquid medications. Using a spoon requires practice. Do not force the liquid down the dog's throat. Position yourself to one side of the dog (I always tackle jobs like this by positioning the dog between me and the wall or counter), and with thumb and forefinger, pull the cheek away from the molars, tilting the chin up. Pour the prescribed dose into the pouch formed by the cheek and teeth. The dog will swallow, and the liquid goes down the correct passageway.

Bleeding

Uncontrolled bleeding is frightening to observe. If the blood is bright red and spurting, it is arterial. If it's dark red and oozing, it is venous. There is often a combination of the two. A pressure dressing of several pieces of clean gauze (or whatever you can grab in an emergency) should be placed over the wound and held or bandaged snugly. Summon help. It is unrealistic to expect a one-hundred-pound woman to be able to carry a one-hundred-pound dog that has suffered an injury. If you carry a blanket in your car, use it to transport the dog, especially if there is more than one person—but don't use this method for a possible spinal injury, in which case you have to keep the dog as still as possible.

Preparing to give a Rottweiler a pill.

Probably the greatest danger your dog faces is from vehicles. Dogs never learn to be reliably traffic conscious. Do not permit your dog to be on a traveled road without a leash. Years ago I was addressing a group of police canine handlers about normal maintenance for their dogs. I talked about bloat, torsion, ruptured cruciate ligaments and so forth. When we broke for coffee later, one of the young officers said to me in a wistful voice, "I was a lot happier before I knew all this stuff." Although it may be true that ignorance is bliss, it's certainly not protection. Knowing what needs to be done to keep your Rottweiler safe and well will add immeasurably to your enjoyment of your canine friend, who is dependent on you.

Your Happy, Healthy Pet

Your Dog's Name _____

Name on Your Dog's Pedigree (if your dog has one) _____

_____

Where Your Dog Came From _____

_____

Your Dog's Birthday _____

Your Dog's Veterinarian

    Name _____

    Address _____

    Phone Number_____

    Emergency Number_____

Your Dog's Health

    Vaccines

    type _____ date given _____

    type _____ date given _____

    type _____ date given _____

    type _____ date given _____

    Heartworm

    date tested _____ type used_____ start date _____

Your Dog's License Number_____

Groomer's Name and Number _____

Dogsitter/Walker's Name and Number_____

Awards Your Dog Has Won

    Award _____ date earned _____

    Award _____ date earned _____

part three

Enjoying
your
Dog

chapter 8

Basic
Training

by Ian Dunbar, Ph.D., MRCVS

Training is the jewel in the crown—the most important aspect of doggy husbandry. There is no more important variable influencing dog behavior and temperament than the dog's education: A well-trained, well-behaved and good-natured puppydog is always a joy to live with, but an untrained and uncivilized dog can be a perpetual nightmare. Moreover, deny the dog an education and it will not have the opportunity to fulfill its own canine potential; neither will it have the ability to communicate effectively with its human companions.

Luckily, modern psychological training methods are easy, efficient and effective and, above all, considerably dog-friendly and user-friendly. Doggy education is as simple as it is enjoyable. But before you can have a good time play-training with your new dog, you have to learn what to do and how to do it. There is no bigger variable influencing the success of dog training than the *owner's* experience and expertise. *Before you embark on the dog's education, you must first educate yourself.*

Basic Training for Owners

Ideally, basic owner training should begin well *before* you select your dog. Find out all you can about your chosen breed first, then master rudimentary training and handling skills. If you already have your puppy/dog, owner training is a dire emergency—the clock is running! Especially for puppies, the first few weeks at home are the most important and influential days in the dog's life. Indeed, the cause of most adolescent and adult problems may be traced back to the initial days the pup explores his new home. This is the time to establish the *status quo*—to teach the puppy/dog how you would like him to behave and so prevent otherwise quite predictable problems.

In addition to consulting breeders and breed books such as this one (which understandably have a positive breed bias), seek out as many pet owners with your breed you can find. Good points are obvious. What you want to find out are the breed-specific *problems,* so you can nip them in the bud. In particular, you should talk to owners with *adolescent* dogs and make a list of all anticipated problems. Most important, *test drive* at least half a dozen adolescent and adult dogs of your breed yourself. An eight-week-old puppy is deceptively easy to handle, but she will acquire adult size, speed and strength in just four months, so you should learn now what to prepare for.

Puppy and pet dog training classes offer a convenient venue to locate pet owners and observe dogs in action. For a list of suitable trainers in your area, contact the Association of Pet Dog Trainers (see Chapter 13). You may also begin your basic owner training by observing other owners in class. Watch as many classes and test drive as many dogs as possible. Select an upbeat, dog-friendly, people-friendly, fun-and-games, puppydog pet training class to learn the ropes. Also, watch training videos and read training books (see Chapter 12). You must find out what to do and how to do it *before* you have to do it.

Principles of Training

Most people think training comprises teaching the dog to do things such as sit, speak and roll over, but even a four-week-old pup knows how to do these things already. Instead, the first step in training involves teaching the dog human words for each dog behavior and activity and for each aspect of the dog's environment. That way you, the owner, can more easily participate in the dog's domestic education by directing him to perform specific actions appropriately, that is, at the right time, in the right place, and so on. Training opens communication channels, enabling an educated dog to at least understand the owner's requests.

In addition to teaching a dog *what* we want her to do, it is also necessary to teach her *why* she should do what we ask. Indeed, 95 percent of training revolves around motivating the dog *to want to do* what we want. Dogs often understand what their owners want; they just don't see the point of doing it—especially when the owner's repetitively boring and seemingly senseless instructions are totally at odds with much more pressing and exciting doggy distractions. It is not so much the dog who is being stubborn or dominant; rather, it is the owner who has failed to acknowledge the dog's needs and feelings and to approach training from the dog's point of view.

The Meaning of Instructions

The secret to successful training is learning how to use training lures to predict or prompt specific behaviors—to coax the dog to do what you want *when* you want. Any highly valued object (such as a treat or toy) may be used as a lure, which the dog will follow with his eyes and nose. Moving the lure in specific ways entices the dog to move his nose, head and entire body in specific ways. In fact, by learning the art of manipulating various lures, it is possible to teach the dog to assume virtually any body position and perform any action. Once you have control over the expression of the dog's behaviors and can elicit any body position or behavior at will, you can easily teach the dog to perform on request.

Tell your dog what you want him to do, use a lure to entice him to respond correctly, then profusely praise

Teach your dog words for each activity he needs to know, like down.

and maybe reward him once he performs the desired action. For example, verbally request "Fido, sit!" while you move a squeaky toy upwards and backwards over the dog's muzzle (lure-movement and hand signal), smile knowingly as he looks up (to follow the lure) and sits down (as a result of canine anatomical engineering), then praise him to distraction ("Gooood Fido!"). Squeak the toy, offer a training treat and give your dog and yourself a pat on the back.

Being able to elicit desired responses over and over enables the owner to reward the dog over and over. Consequently, the dog begins to think training is fun. For example, the more the dog is rewarded for sitting, the more she enjoys sitting. Eventually the dog comes to realize that, whereas most sitting is appreciated, sitting immediately upon request usually prompts especially enthusiastic praise and a slew of high-level rewards. The dog begins to sit on cue much of the time, showing that she is starting to grasp the meaning of the owner's verbal request and hand signal.

Why Comply?

Most dogs enjoy initial lure/reward training and are only too happy to comply with their owners' wishes. Unfortunately, repetitive drilling without appreciative feedback tends to diminish the dog's enthusiasm until he eventually fails to see the point of complying anymore. Moreover, as the dog approaches adolescence he becomes more easily distracted as he develops other interests. Lengthy sessions with repetitive exercises tend to bore and demotivate both parties. If it's not fun, the owner doesn't do it and neither does the dog.

Integrate training into your dog's life: The greater number of training sessions each day and the *shorter* they are, the more willingly compliant your dog will become. Make sure to have a short (just a few seconds) training interlude before every enjoyable canine activity. For example, ask your dog to sit to greet people, to sit before you throw his Frisbee, and to sit for his supper. Really, sitting is no different from a canine "please." Also, include numerous short training interludes during every enjoyable canine pastime, for example, when playing with the dog or when he is running in the park. In this fashion, doggy distractions may be effectively converted into rewards for training. Just as all games have rules, fun becomes training . . . and training becomes fun.

Eventually, rewards actually become unnecessary to continue motivating your dog. If trained with consideration and kindness, performing the desired behaviors will become self-rewarding and, in a sense, your dog will motivate himself. Just as it is not necessary to reward a human companion during an enjoyable walk in the park, or following a game of tennis, it is hardly necessary to reward our best friend—the dog—for walking by our side or while playing fetch. Human company during enjoyable activities is reward enough for most dogs.

Even though your dog has become self-motivating, it's still good to praise and pet him a lot and offer rewards once in a while, especially for a good job well done. And if for no other reason, praising and rewarding others is good for the human heart.

To train your dog, you need gentle hands, a loving heart and a good attitude.

Punishment

Without a doubt, lure/reward training is by far the best way to teach: Entice your dog to do what you want and then reward him for doing so. Unfortunately, a human shortcoming is to take the good for granted and to moan and groan at the bad. Specifically, the dog's many good behaviors are ignored while the owner focuses on punishing the dog for making mistakes. In extreme cases, instruction is *limited* to punishing mistakes made by a trainee dog, child, employee or husband, even though it has been proven punishment training is notoriously inefficient and ineffective and is decidedly unfriendly and combative. It teaches the dog that training is a drag, almost as quickly as it teaches the dog to dislike his trainer. Why treat our best friends like our worst enemies?

Punishment training is also much more laborious and time consuming. Whereas it takes only a finite amount of time to teach a dog what to chew, for example, it takes much, much longer to punish the dog for each and every mistake. Remember, *there is only one right way!* So why not teach that right way from the outset?!

To make matters worse, punishment training causes severe lapses in the dog's reliability. Since it is obviously impossible to punish the dog each and every time she misbehaves, the dog quickly learns to distinguish between those times when she must comply (so as to avoid impending punishment) and those times when she need not comply, because punishment is impossible. Such times include when the dog is off leash and only six feet away, when the owner is otherwise engaged (talking to a friend, watching television, taking a shower, tending to the baby or chatting on the telephone), or when the dog is left at home alone.

Instances of misbehavior will be numerous when the owner is away, because even when the dog complied in the owner's looming presence, he did so unwillingly. The dog was forced to act against his will, rather than moulding his will to want to please. Hence, when the owner is absent, not only does the dog know he need not comply, he simply does not want to. Again, the trainee is not a stubborn vindictive beast, but rather the trainer has failed to teach.

Punishment training invariably creates unpredictable Jekyll and Hyde behavior.

Trainer's Tools

Many training books extol the virtues of a vast array of training paraphernalia and electronic and metallic gizmos, most of which are designed for canine restraint, correction and punishment, rather than for actual facilitation of doggy education. In reality, most effective training tools are not found in stores; they come from within ourselves. In addition to a willing dog, all you really need is a functional human brain, gentle hands, a loving heart and a good attitude.

In terms of equipment, all dogs do require a quality buckle collar to sport dog tags and to attach the leash (for safety and to comply with local leash laws). Hollow chewtoys (like Kongs or sterilized longbones) and a dog bed or collapsible crate are a must for housetraining. Three additional tools are required:

1. specific lures (training treats and toys) to predict and prompt specific desired behaviors;

2. rewards (praise, affection, training treats and toys) to reinforce for the dog what a lot of fun it all is; and

3. knowledge—how to convert the dog's favorite activities and games (potential distractions to training) into "life-rewards," which may be employed to facilitate training.

The most powerful of these is *knowledge*. Education is the key! Watch training classes, participate in training classes, watch videos, read books, enjoy playtraining with your dog, and then your dog will say "Please," and your dog will say "Thank you!"

Housetraining

If dogs were left to their own devices, certainly they would chew, dig and bark for entertainment and then no doubt highlight a few areas of their living space with sprinkles of urine, in much the same way we decorate by hanging pictures. Consequently, when we ask a dog to live with us, we must teach him *where* he may dig and perform his toilet duties, *what* he may chew and *when* he may bark. After all, when left at home alone for many hours, we cannot expect the dog to amuse himself by completing crosswords or watching the soaps on TV!

Also, it would be decidedly unfair to keep the house rules a secret from the dog, and then get angry and punish the poor critter for inevitably transgressing rules he did not even know existed. Remember, without adequate education and guidance, the dog will be forced to establish his own rules—doggy rules—that most probably will be at odds with the owner's view of domestic living.

Since most problems develop during the first few days the dog is at home, prospective dog owners must be certain they are quite clear about the principles of housetraining *before* they get a dog. Early misbehaviors quickly become established as the status quo—

becoming firmly entrenched as hard-to-break bad habits, which set the precedent for years to come. Make sure to teach your dog good habits right from the start. Good habits are just as hard to break as bad ones!

Ideally, when a new dog comes home, try to arrange for someone to be present for as much as possible during the first few days (for adult dogs) or weeks for puppies. With only a little forethought, it is surprisingly easy to find a puppy sitter, such as a retired person, who would be willing to eat from your refrigerator and watch your television while keeping an eye on the newcomer to encourage the dog to play with chewtoys and to ensure he goes outside on a regular basis.

POTTY TRAINING

To teach the dog where to relieve himself:

1. never let him make a single mistake;

2. let him know where you want him to go; and

3. handsomely reward him for doing so: "GOOOOOOOD DOG!!!" liver treat, liver treat, liver treat!

PREVENTING MISTAKES

A single mistake is a training disaster, since it heralds many more in future weeks. And each time the dog soils the house, this further reinforces the dog's unfortunate preference for an indoor, carpeted toilet. *Do not let an unhousetrained dog have full run of the house if you are away from home or cannot pay full attention.* Instead, confine the dog to an area where elimination is appropriate, such as an outdoor run or, better still, a small, comfortable indoor kennel with access to an outdoor run. When confined in this manner, most dogs will naturally housetrain themselves.

If that's not possible, confine the dog to an area, such as a utility room, kitchen, basement or garage, where elimination may not be desired in the long run but as an interim measure it is certainly preferable to doing it all around the house. Use newspaper to cover the floor of the dog's day room. The newspaper may be used to soak up the urine and to wrap up and dispose of the feces. Once your dog develops a preferred spot for eliminating, it is only necessary to cover that part of the floor with newspaper. The smaller papered area may then be moved (only a little each day) towards the door to the outside. Thus the dog will develop the tendency to go to the door when he needs to relieve himself.

The first few weeks at home are the most important and influential in your dog's life.

Never confine an unhousetrained dog to a crate for long periods. Doing so would force the dog to soil the crate and ruin its usefulness as an aid for housetraining (see the following discussion).

Teaching Where

In order to teach your dog where you would like her to do her business, you have to be there to direct the proceedings—an obvious, yet often neglected, fact of life. In order to be there to teach the dog *where* to go, you need to know *when* she needs to go. Indeed, the success of housetraining depends on the owner's ability to predict these times. Certainly, a regular feeding schedule will facilitate prediction somewhat, but there is

nothing like "loading the deck" and influencing the timing of the outcome yourself!

Whenever you are at home, make sure the dog is under constant supervision and/or confined to a small area. If already well trained, simply instruct the dog to lie down in his bed or basket. Alternatively, confine the dog to a crate (doggy den) or tie-down (a short, 18-inch lead that can be clipped to an eye hook in the baseboard). Short-term close confinement strongly inhibits urination and defecation, since the dog does not want to soil his sleeping area. Thus, when you release the puppydog each hour, he will definitely need to urinate immediately and defecate every third or fourth hour. Keep the dog confined to his doggy den and take him to his intended toilet area each hour, every hour, and on the hour.

When taking your dog outside, instruct him to sit quietly before opening the door—he will soon learn to sit by the door when he needs to go out!

TEACHING WHY

Being able to predict when the dog needs to go enables the owner to be on the spot to praise and reward the dog. Each hour, hurry the dog to the intended toilet area in the yard, issue the appropriate instruction ("Go pee!" or "Go poop!"), then give the dog three to four minutes to produce. Praise and offer a couple of training treats when successful. The treats are important because many people fail to praise their dogs with feeling . . . and housetraining is hardly the time for understatement. So either loosen up and enthusiastically praise that dog: "Wuzzzer-wuzzer-wuzzer, hoooser good wuffer den? Hoooo went pee for Daddy?" Or say "Good dog!" as best you can and offer the treats for effect.

Following elimination is an ideal time for a spot of playtraining in the yard or house. Also, an empty dog may be allowed greater freedom around the house for the next half hour or so, just as long as you keep an eye out to make sure he does not get into other kinds of mischief. If you are preoccupied and cannot pay full attention, confine the dog to his doggy den once more to enjoy a peaceful snooze or to play with his many chewtoys.

If your dog does not eliminate within the allotted time outside—no biggie! Back to his doggy den, and then try again after another hour.

As I own large dogs, I always feel more relaxed walking an empty dog, knowing that I will not need to finish our stroll weighted down with bags of feces! Beware of falling into the trap of walking the dog to get it to eliminate. The good ol' dog walk is such an enormous highlight in the dog's life that it represents the single biggest potential reward in domestic dogdom. However, when in a hurry, or during inclement weather, many owners abruptly terminate the walk the moment the dog has done its business. This, in effect, severely punishes the dog for doing the right thing, in the right place at the right time. Consequently, many dogs become strongly inhibited from eliminating outdoors because they know it will signal an abrupt end to an otherwise thoroughly enjoyable walk.

Instead, instruct the dog to relieve himself in the yard prior to going for a walk. If you follow the above instructions, most dogs soon learn to eliminate on cue. As soon as the dog eliminates, praise (and offer a treat or two)—"Good dog! Let's go walkies!" Use the walk as a reward for eliminating in the yard. If the dog does not go, put him back in his doggy den and think about a walk later on. You will find with a "No feces–no walk" policy, your dog will become one of the fastest defecators in the business.

If you do not have a back yard, instruct the dog to eliminate right outside your front door prior to the walk. Not only will this facilitate clean up and disposal of the feces in your own trash can but, also, the walk may again be used as a colossal reward.

CHEWING AND BARKING

Short-term close confinement also teaches the dog that occasional quiet moments are a reality of domestic living. Your puppydog is extremely impressionable during his first few weeks at home. Regular confinement at this time soon exerts a calming influence over the dog's personality. Remember, once the dog is housetrained and calmer, there will be a whole lifetime ahead for the dog to enjoy full run of the house and garden. On the other hand, by letting the newcomer have unrestricted access to the entire household and allowing him to run willy-nilly, he will most certainly develop a bunch of behavior problems in short order, no doubt necessitating confinement later in life. It would not be fair to remedially restrain and confine a dog you have trained, through neglect, to run free.

When confining the dog, make sure he always has an impressive array of suitable chewtoys. Kongs and sterilized longbones (both readily available from pet stores) make the best chewtoys, since they are hollow and may be stuffed with treats to heighten the dog's interest. For example, by stuffing the little hole at the top of a Kong with a small piece of freeze-dried liver, the dog will not want to leave it alone.

Remember, treats do not have to be junk food and they certainly should not represent extra calories. Rather, treats should be part of each dog's regular daily diet:

Make sure your puppy has suitable chewtoys.

Some food may be served in the dog's bowl for breakfast and dinner, some food may be used as training treats, and some food may be used for stuffing chewtoys. I regularly stuff my dogs' many Kongs with different shaped biscuits and kibble. The kibble seems to fall out fairly easily, as do the oval-shaped biscuits, thus rewarding the dog instantaneously for checking out the chewtoys. The bone-shaped biscuits fall out after a while, rewarding the dog for worrying at the chewtoy. But the triangular biscuits never come out. They remain inside the Kong as lures, maintaining the dog's fascination with its chewtoy. To further focus the dog's interest, I always make sure to flavor the triangular biscuits by rubbing them with a little cheese or freeze-dried liver.

If stuffed chewtoys are reserved especially for times the dog is confined, the puppy-dog will soon learn to enjoy quiet moments in her doggy den and she will quickly develop a chewtoy habit—a good habit! This is a simple *passive training* process; all the owner has to do is set up the situation and the dog all but trains herself—easy and effective. Even when the dog is given run of the house, her first inclination will be to indulge her rewarding chewtoy habit rather than destroying less-attractive household articles, such as curtains, carpets, chairs and compact disks. Similarly, a chewtoy chewer will be less inclined to scratch and chew herself excessively. Also, if the dog busies herself as a recreational chewer, she will be less inclined to develop into a recreational barker or digger when left at home alone.

Stuff a number of chewtoys whenever the dog is left confined and remove the extra-special-tasting treats when you return. Your dog will now amuse himself with his chewtoys before falling asleep and then resume playing with his chewtoys when he expects you to return. Since most owner-absent misbehavior happens right after you leave and right before your expected return, your puppydog will now be conveniently preoccupied with his chewtoys at these times.

To teach come, call your dog, open your arms as a welcoming signal, wave a toy or a treat and praise for every step in your direction.

Come and Sit

Most puppies will happily approach virtually anyone, whether called or not; that is, until they collide with adolescence and develop other more important doggy interests, such as sniffing a multiplicity of exquisite odors on the grass. Your mission, Mr. and/or Ms. Owner, is to teach and reward the pup for coming reliably, willingly and happily when called—and you have just three months to get it done. Unless adequately reinforced, your puppy's tendency to approach people will self-destruct by adolescence.

Call your dog ("Fido, come!"), open your arms (and maybe squat down) as a welcoming signal, waggle a treat or toy as a lure, and reward the puppydog when he comes running. Do not wait to praise the dog until he reaches you—he may come 95 percent of the way and then run off after some distraction. Instead, praise the dog's *first* step towards you and continue praising enthusiastically for *every* step he takes in your direction.

When the rapidly approaching puppy dog is three lengths away from impact, instruct him to sit ("Fido, sit!") and hold the lure in front of you in an outstretched hand to prevent him from hitting you midchest and knocking you flat on your back! As Fido decelerates to nose the lure, move the treat upwards and backwards just over his muzzle with an upwards motion of your extended arm (palm-upwards). As the dog looks up to follow the lure, he will sit down (if he jumps up, you are holding the lure too high). Praise the dog for sitting. Move backwards and call him again. Repeat this many times over, always praising when Fido comes and sits; on occasion, reward him.

For the first couple of trials, use a training treat both as a lure to entice the dog to come and sit and as a reward for doing so. Thereafter, try to use different items as lures and rewards. For example, lure the dog with a Kong or Frisbee but reward her with a food treat. Or lure the dog with a food treat but pat her and throw a tennis ball as a reward. After just a few repetitions, dispense with the lures and rewards; the dog will begin to respond willingly to your verbal requests and hand signals just for the prospect of praise from your heart and affection from your hands.

Instruct every family member, friend and visitor how to get the dog to come and sit. Invite people over for a series of pooch parties; do not keep the pup a secret— let other people enjoy this puppy, and let the pup enjoy other people. Puppydog parties are not only fun, they easily attract a lot of people to help *you* train *your* dog. Unless you teach your dog *how* to meet people, that is, to sit for greetings, no doubt the dog will resort to jumping up. Then you and the visitors will get annoyed, and the dog will be punished. This is not fair. *Send out those invitations for puppy parties and teach your dog to be mannerly and socially acceptable.*

Even though your dog quickly masters obedient recalls in the house, his reliability may falter when playing in the back yard or local park. Ironically, it is *the owner* who has unintentionally trained the dog *not* to respond in these instances. By allowing the dog to play and run around and otherwise have a good time, but then to call the dog to put him on leash to take him home, the dog quickly learns playing is fun but training is a drag. Thus, playing in the park becomes a severe distraction, which works against training. Bad news!

Instead, whether playing with the dog off leash or on leash, request him to come at frequent intervals— say, every minute or so. On most occasions, praise and pet the dog for a few seconds while he is sitting, then tell him to go play again. For especially fast recalls, offer a couple of training treats and take the time to praise and pet the dog enthusiastically before releasing him. The dog will learn that coming when called is not necessarily the end of the play session, and neither is it the end of the world; rather, it signals an enjoyable, quality time-out with the owner before resuming play once more. In fact, playing in the park now becomes a very effective life-reward, which works to facilitate training by reinforcing each obedient and timely recall. Good news!

Sit, Down, Stand and Rollover

Teaching the dog a variety of body positions is easy for owner and dog, impressive for spectators and extremely useful for all. Using lure-reward techniques, it is possible to train several positions at once to verbal commands or hand signals (which impress the socks off onlookers).

Sit and *down*—the two control commands—prevent or resolve nearly a hundred behavior problems. For example, if the dog happily and obediently sits or lies down when requested, he cannot jump on visitors, dash out the front door, run around and chase its tail, pester other dogs, harass cats or annoy family, friends or strangers. Additionally, "sit" or "down" are better emergency commands for off-leash control.

It is easier to teach and maintain a reliable sit than maintain a reliable recall. *Sit* is the purest and simplest of commands—either the dog is sitting or he is not. If there is any change of circumstances or potential danger in the park, for example, simply instruct the dog to sit. If he sits, you have a number of options: allow the dog to resume playing when he is safe; walk up and put the dog on leash, or call the dog. The dog will be much more likely to come when called if he has already acknowledged his compliance by sitting. If the dog does not sit in the park—train him to!

Stand and *rollover-stay* are the two positions for examining the dog. Your veterinarian will love you to distraction if you take a little time to teach the dog to stand still and roll over and play possum. Also, your vet bills will be smaller. The rollover-stay is an especially useful command and is really just a variation of the down-stay: whereas the dog lies prone in the traditional down, she lies supine in the rollover-stay.

As with teaching come and sit, the training techniques to teach the dog to assume all other body positions on cue are user-friendly and dog-friendly. Simply give the appropriate request, lure the dog into the desired body position using a training treat or toy and then *praise* (and maybe reward) the dog as soon as he complies. Try not to touch the dog to get him to respond. If you teach the dog by guiding him into position, the dog will quickly learn that rump-pressure means sit, for example, but as yet you still have no control over your dog if he is just six feet away. It will still be necessary to teach the dog to sit on request. So do not make training a time-consuming two-step process; instead, teach the dog to sit to a verbal request or hand signal from the outset. Once the dog sits willingly when requested, by all means use your hands to pet the dog when he does so.

To teach *down* when the dog is already sitting, say "Fido, down!," hold the lure in one hand (palm down) and lower that hand to the floor between the dog's forepaws. As the dog lowers his head to follow the lure, slowly move the lure away from the dog just a fraction (in front of his paws). The dog will lie down as he stretches his nose forward to follow the lure. Praise the dog when he does so. If the dog stands up, you pulled the lure away too far and too quickly.

When teaching the dog to lie down from the standing position, say "down" and lower the lure to the floor as before. Once the dog has lowered his forequarters and assumed a play bow, gently and slowly move the lure *towards* the dog between his forelegs. Praise the dog as soon as his rear end plops down.

After just a couple of trials it will be possible to alternate sits and downs and have the dog energetically perform doggy push-ups. Praise the dog a lot, and after half a dozen or so push-ups reward the dog with a training treat or toy. You will notice the more energetically you move your arm—upwards (palm up) to get the dog to sit, and downwards (palm down) to get the dog to lie down—the more energetically the dog responds to your requests. Now try training the dog in silence and you will notice he has also learned to respond to hand signals. Yeah! Not too shabby for the first session.

To teach *stand* from the sitting position, say "Fido, stand," slowly move the lure half a dog-length away from the dog's nose, keeping it at nose level, and praise the dog as he stands to follow the lure. As soon

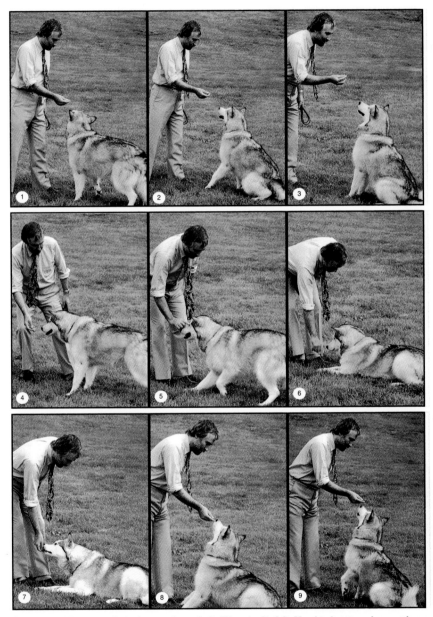

Using a food lure to teach sit, down and stand. 1) "Phoenix, Sit." 2) Hand palm upwards, move lure up and back over dog's muzzle. 3) "Good sit, Phoenix!" 4) "Phoenix, down." 5) Hand palm downwards, move lure down to lie between dog's forepaws. 6) "Phoenix, off. Good down, Phoenix!" 7) "Phoenix, sit!" 8) Palm upwards, move lure up and back, keeping it close to dog's muzzle. 9) "Good sit, Phoenix!"

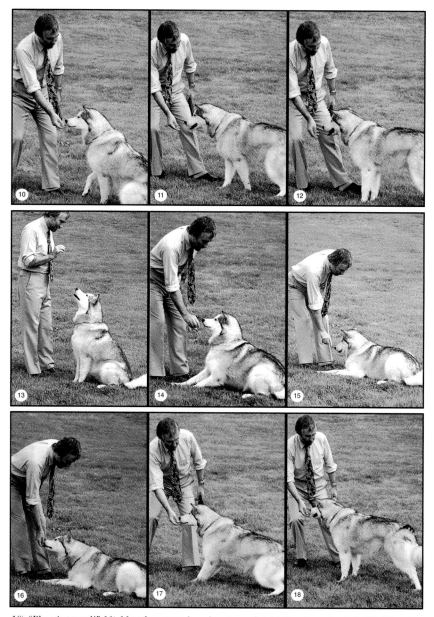

10) *"Phoenix, stand!"* 11) *Move lure away from dog at nose height, then lower it a tad.* 12) *"Phoenix, off! Good stand, Phoenix!"* 13) *"Phoenix, down!"* 14) *Hand palm downwards, move lure down to lie between dog's forepaws.* 15) *"Phoenix, off! Good down-stay, Phoenix!"* 16) *"Phoenix, stand!"* 17) *Move lure away from dog's muzzle up to nose height.* 18) *"Phoenix, off! Good stand-stay, Phoenix. Now we'll make the vet and groomer happy!"*

as the dog stands, lower the lure to just beneath the dog's chin to entice him to look down; otherwise he will stand and then sit immediately. To prompt the dog to stand from the down position, move the lure half a dog-length upwards and away from the dog, holding the lure at standing nose height from the floor.

Teaching *rollover* is best started from the down position, with the dog lying on one side, or at least with both hind legs stretched out on the same side. Say "Fido, bang!" and move the lure backwards and alongside the dog's muzzle to its elbow (on the side of its outstretched hind legs). Once the dog looks to the side and backwards, very slowly move the lure upwards to the dog's shoulder and backbone. Tickling the dog in the goolies (groin area) often invokes a reflex-raising of the hind leg as an appeasement gesture, which facilitates the tendency to roll over. If you move the lure too quickly and the dog jumps into the standing position, have patience and start again. As soon as the dog rolls onto its back, keep the lure stationary and mesmerize the dog with a relaxing tummy rub.

To teach *rollover-stay* when the dog is standing or moving, say "Fido, bang!" and give the appropriate hand signal (with index finger pointed and thumb cocked in true Sam Spade fashion), then in one fluid movement lure him to first lie down and then rollover-stay as above.

Teaching the dog to *stay* in each of the above four positions becomes a piece of cake after first teaching the dog not to worry at the toy or treat training lure. This is best accomplished by hand feeding dinner kibble. Hold a piece of kibble firmly in your hand and softly instruct "Off!" Ignore any licking and slobbering *for however long the dog worries at the treat,* but say "Take it!" and offer the kibble *the instant* the dog breaks contact with his muzzle. Repeat this a few times, and then up the ante and insist the dog remove his muzzle for one whole second before offering the kibble. Then progressively refine your criteria and have the dog not touch your hand (or treat) for longer and longer periods on each trial, such as for two seconds, four seconds, then six, ten, fifteen, twenty, thirty seconds and so on. The dog soon learns: (1) worrying at the treat never gets results, whereas (2) noncontact is often rewarded after a variable time lapse.

Teaching *"Off!"* has many useful applications in its own right. Additionally, instructing the dog not to touch a training lure often produces spontaneous and magical stays. Request the dog to stand-stay, for example, and not to touch the lure. At first set your sights on a short two-second stay before rewarding the dog. (Remember, every long journey begins with a single step.) However, on subsequent trials, gradually and progressively increase the length of stay required to receive a reward. In no time at all your dog will stand calmly for a minute or so.

Relevancy Training

Once you have taught the dog what you expect her to do when requested to come, sit, lie down, stand, rollover and stay, the time is right to teach the dog *why* she should comply with your wishes. The secret is to have many (*many*) extremely short training interludes (two to five seconds each) at numerous (*numerous*) times during the course of the dog's day. Especially work with the dog immediately *before* the dog's good times and *during* the dog's good times. For example, ask your dog to sit and/or lie down each time before opening doors, serving meals, offering treats and tummy rubs; ask the dog to perform a few controlled doggy push-ups before letting her off-leash or throwing a tennis ball; and perhaps request the dog to sit-down-sit-stand-down-stand-rollover before inviting her to cuddle on the couch.

Similarly, request the dog to sit many times during play or on walks, and in no time at all the dog will be only too pleased to follow your instructions because he has learned that a compliant response heralds all sorts of goodies. Basically all you are trying to teach the dog is how to say please: "Please throw the tennis ball. Please may I snuggle on the couch."

Remember, whereas it is important to keep training interludes short, it is equally important to have many short sessions each and every day. The shortest (and most useful) session comprises asking the dog to sit and then go play during a play session. When trained this way, your dog will soon associate training with good times. In fact, the dog may be unable to distinguish between training and good times and, indeed, there should be no distinction. The warped concept that training involves forcing the dog to comply and/or dominating his will is totally at odds with the picture of a truly well-trained dog. In reality, enjoying a game of training with a dog is no different from enjoying a game of backgammon or tennis with a friend; and walking with a dog should be no different from strolling with buddies on the golf course.

Walk by Your Side

Many people attempt to teach a dog to heel by putting him on a leash and physically correcting the dog when he makes mistakes. There are a number of things seriously wrong with this approach, the first being that most people do not want precision heeling; rather, they simply want the dog to follow or walk by their side. Second, when physically restrained during "training," even though the dog may grudgingly mope by your side when "handcuffed" on leash, let's see what happens when he is off leash. History! The dog is in the next county because he never enjoyed walking with you on leash and you have no control over him off leash. So let's just teach the dog off leash from the outset to *want* to walk with us. Third, if the dog has not been trained to heel, it is a trifle hasty to think about punishing the poor dog for making mistakes and breaking heeling rules he didn't even know existed. This is simply not fair! Surely, if the dog had been adequately taught how to heel, he would seldom make mistakes and hence there would be no need to correct the dog. Remember, each mistake and each correction (punishment) advertise the trainer's inadequacy, not the dog's. The dog is not stubborn, he is not stupid and he is not bad. Even if he were, he would still require training, so let's train him properly.

Let's teach the dog to *enjoy* following us and to *want* to walk by our side offleash. Then it will be easier to teach high-precision off-leash heeling patterns if desired. After attaching the leash for safety on outdoor walks, but before going anywhere, it is necessary to teach the dog specifically not to pull. Now it will be much easier to teach on-leash walking and heeling because the dog already wants to walk with you, he is familiar with the desired walking and heeling positions and he knows not to pull.

FOLLOWING

Start by training your dog to follow you. Many puppies will follow if you simply walk away from them and maybe click your fingers or chuckle. Adult dogs may require additional enticement to stimulate them to follow, such as a training lure or, at the very least, a lively trainer. To teach the dog to follow: (1) keep walking and (2) walk away from the dog. If the dog attempts to lead or lag, change pace; slow down if the dog forges too far ahead, but speed up if he lags too far behind. Say "Steady!" or "Easy!" each time before you slow down and "Quickly!" or "Hustle!" each time before you speed up, and the dog will learn to change pace on cue. If the dog lags or leads too far, or if he wanders right or left, simply walk quickly in the opposite direction and maybe even run away from the dog and hide.

Practicing is a lot of fun; you can set up a course in your home, yard or park to do this. Indoors, entice the dog to follow upstairs, into a bedroom, into the bathroom, downstairs, around the living room couch, zigzagging between dining room chairs and into the kitchen for dinner. Outdoors, get the dog to follow around park benches, trees, shrubs and along walkways and lines in the grass. (For safety outdoors, it is advisable to attach a long line on the dog, but never exert corrective tension on the line.)

Remember, following has a lot to do with attitude—*your* attitude! Most probably your dog will *not* want to follow Mr. Grumpy Troll with the personality of wilted lettuce. Lighten up—walk with a jaunty step, whistle a happy tune, sing, skip and tell jokes to your dog and he will be right there by your side.

BY YOUR SIDE

It is smart to train the dog to walk close on one side or the other—either side will do, your choice. When walking, jogging or cycling, it is generally bad news to have the dog suddenly cut in front of you. In fact, I train my dogs to walk "By my side" and "Other side"—both very useful instructions. It is possible to position the dog fairly accurately by looking to the appropriate side and clicking your fingers or slapping your thigh on that side. A precise positioning may be attained by holding a training lure, such as a chewtoy, tennis ball, or food treat. Stop and stand still several times throughout the walk, just as you would when window shopping or meeting a friend. Use the lure to make sure the dog slows down and stays close whenever you stop.

When teaching the dog to heel, we generally want her to sit in heel position when we stop. Teach heel

Using a toy to teach sit-heel-sit sequences: 1) "Phoenix, heel!" Standing still, move lure up and back over dog's muzzle.... 2) To position dog sitting in heel position on your left side. 3) "Phoenix, heel!" wagging lure in left hand. Change lure to right hand in preparation for sit signal.

position at the standstill and the dog will learn that the default heel position is sitting by your side (left or right—your choice, unless you wish to compete in obedience trials, in which case the dog must heel on the left).

Several times a day, stand up and call your dog to come and sit in heel position—"Fido, heel!" For example, instruct the dog to come to heel each time there are commercials on TV, or each time you turn a page of a novel, and the dog will get it in a single evening.

Practice straight-line heeling and turns separately. With the dog sitting at heel, teach him to turn in place. After each quarter-turn, half-turn or full turn in place, lure the dog to sit at heel. Now it's time for short straight-line heeling sequences, no more than a few steps at a time. Always think of heeling in terms of Sit-Heel-Sit sequences—start and end with the dog in position and do your best to keep him there when moving. Progressively increase the number of steps in each sequence. When the dog remains close for 20 yards of straight-line heeling, it is time to add a few turns and then sign up for a happy-heeling obedience class to get some advice from the experts.

4) Use hand signal only to lure dog to sit as you stop. Eventually, dog will sit automatically at heel whenever you stop. 5) "Good dog!"

NO PULLING ON LEASH

You can start teaching your dog not to pull on leash anywhere—in front of the television or outdoors—but regardless of location, you must not take a single step with tension in the leash. For a reason known only to dogs, even just a couple of paces of pulling on leash is intrinsically motivating and diabolically rewarding. Instead, attach the leash to the dog's collar, grasp the other end firmly with both hands held close to your chest, and stand still—do not budge an inch. Have somebody watch you with a stopwatch to time your progress, or else you will never believe this will work and so you will not even try the exercise, and your shoulder and the dog's neck will be traumatized for years to come.

Stand still and wait for the dog to stop pulling, and to sit and/or lie down. All dogs stop pulling and sit eventually. Most take only a couple of minutes; the all-time record is 22 $\frac{1}{5}$ minutes. Time how long it takes. Gently praise the dog when he stops pulling, and as soon as he sits, enthusiastically praise the dog and take just one step forwards, then immediately stand still. This single step usually demonstrates the ballistic reinforcing nature of pulling on leash; most dogs explode to the end of the leash, so be prepared for the strain. Stand firm and wait for the dog to sit again. Repeat this half a dozen times and you will probably notice a progressive reduction in the force of the dog's one-step explosions and a radical reduction in the time it takes for the dog to sit each time.

As the dog learns "Sit we go" and "Pull we stop," she will begin to walk forward calmly with each single step and automatically sit when you stop. Now try two steps before you stop. Wooooooo! Scary! When the dog has mastered two steps at a time, try for three. After each success, progressively increase the number of steps in the sequence: try four steps and then six, eight, ten and twenty steps before stopping. Congratulations! You are now walking the dog on leash.

Whenever walking with the dog (off leash or on leash), make sure you stop periodically to practice a few position commands and stays before instructing the dog to "Walk on!" (Remember, you want the dog to be compliant everywhere, not just in the kitchen when his dinner is at hand.) For example, stopping every 25 yards to briefly train the dog amounts to over 200 training interludes within a single three-mile stroll. And each training session is in a different location. You will not believe the improvement within just the first mile of the first walk.

To put it another way, integrating training into a walk offers 200 separate opportunities to use the continuance of the walk as a reward to reinforce the dog's education. Moreover, some training interludes may comprise continuing education for the dog's walking skills: Alternate short periods of the dog walking calmly by your side with periods when the dog is allowed to sniff and investigate the environment. Now sniffing odors on the grass and meeting other dogs become rewards which reinforce the dog's calm and mannerly demeanor. Good Lord! Whatever next? Many enjoyable walks together of course. Happy trails!

THE IMPORTANCE OF TRICKS

Nothing will improve a dog's quality of life better than having a few tricks under its belt. Teaching any trick expands the dog's vocabulary, which facilitates communication and improves the owner's control. Also, specific tricks help prevent and resolve specific behavior problems. For example, by teaching the dog to fetch his toys, the dog learns carrying a toy makes the owner happy and, therefore, will be more likely to chew his toy than other inappropriate items.

More important, teaching tricks prompts owners to lighten up and train with a sunny disposition. Really, tricks should be no different from any other behaviors we put on cue. But they are. When teaching tricks, owners have a much sweeter attitude, which in turn motivates the dog and improves her willingness to comply. The dog feels tricks are a blast, but formal commands are a drag. In fact, tricks are so enjoyable, they may be used as rewards in training by asking the dog to come, sit and down-stay and then rollover for a tummy rub. Go on, try it: Crack a smile and even giggle when the dog promptly and willingly lies down and stays.

Most important, performing tricks prompts onlookers to smile and giggle. Many people are scared of dogs, especially large ones. And nothing can be more off-putting for a dog than to be constantly confronted by strangers who don't like him because of his size or the way he looks. Uneasy people put the dog on edge, causing him to back off and bark, only frightening people all the more. And so a vicious circle develops, with the people's fear fueling the dog's fear *and vice versa*. Instead, tie a pink ribbon to your dog's collar and practice all sorts of tricks on walks and in the park, and you will be pleasantly amazed how it changes people's attitudes toward your friendly dog. The dog's repertoire of tricks is limited only by the trainer's imagination. Below I have described three of my favorites:

SPEAK AND SHUSH

The training sequence involved in teaching a dog to bark on request is no different from that used when training any behavior on cue: request—lure—response—reward. As always, the secret of success lies in finding an effective lure. If the dog always barks at the doorbell, for example, say "Rover, speak!", have an accomplice ring the doorbell, then reward the dog for barking. After a few woofs, ask Rover to "Shush!", waggle a food treat under his nose (to entice him to sniff and thus to shush), praise him when quiet and eventually offer the treat as a reward. Alternate "Speak" and "Shush," progressively increasing the length of shush-time between each barking bout.

PLAYBOW

With the dog standing, say "Bow!" and lower the food lure (palm upwards) to rest between the dog's forepaws. Praise as the dog lowers her forequarters and sternum to the ground (as when teaching the down), but then lure the dog to stand and offer the treat. On successive trials, gradually increase the length of time the dog is required to remain in the playbow posture in order to gain a food reward. If the dog's rear end collapses into a down, say nothing and offer no reward; simply start over.

BE A BEAR

With the dog sitting backed into a corner to prevent him from toppling over backwards, say "Be a Bear!" With bent paw and palm down, raise a lure upwards and backwards along the top of the dog's muzzle. Praise the dog when he sits up on his haunches and offer the treat as a reward. To prevent the dog from standing on his hind legs, keep the lure closer to the dog's muzzle. On each trial, progressively increase the length of time the dog is required to sit up to receive a food reward. Since lure/reward training is so easy, teach the dog to stand and walk on his hind legs as well!

Teaching "Be a Bear"

chapter 9

Getting
Active
with your Dog

by Bardi McLennan

Once you and your dog have graduated from basic obedience training and are beginning to work together as a team, you can take part in the growing world of dog activities. There are so many fun things to do with your dog! Just remember, people and dogs don't always learn at the same pace, so don't be upset if you (or your dog) need more than two basic training courses before your team becomes operational. Even smart dogs don't go straight to college from kindergarten!

Just as there are events geared to certain types of dogs, so there are ones that are more appealing to certain types of people. In some

128

activities, you give the commands and your dog does the work (upland game hunting is one example), while in others, such as agility, you'll both get a workout. You may want to aim for prestigious titles to add to your dog's name, or you may want nothing more than the sheer enjoyment of being around other people and their dogs. Passive or active, participation has its own rewards.

Consider your dog's physical capabilities when looking into any of the canine activities. It's easy to see that a Basset Hound is not built for the racetrack, nor would a Chihuahua be the breed of choice for pulling a sled. A loyal dog will attempt almost anything you ask him to do, so it is up to you to know your dog's limitations. A dog must be physically sound in order to compete at any level in athletic activities, and being mentally sound is a definite plus. Advanced age, however, may not be a deterrent. Many dogs still hunt and herd at ten or twelve years of age. It's entirely possible for dogs to be "fit at 50." Take your dog for a checkup, explain to your vet the type of activity you have in mind and be guided by his or her findings.

All dogs seem to love playing flyball.

You needn't be restricted to breed-specific sports if it's only fun you're after. Certain AKC activities are limited to designated breeds; however, as each new trial, test or sport has grown in popularity, so has the variety of breeds encouraged to participate at a fun level.

But don't shortchange your fun, or that of your dog, by thinking only of the basic function of her breed. Once a dog has learned how to learn, she can be taught to do just about anything as long as the size of the dog is right for the job and you both think it is fun and rewarding. In other words, you are a team.

To get involved in any of the activities detailed in this chapter, look for the names and addresses of the organizations that sponsor them in Chapter 13. You can also ask your breeder or a local dog trainer for contacts.

You can compete in obedience trials with a well trained dog.

Official American Kennel Club Activities

The following tests and trials are some of the events sanctioned by the AKC and sponsored by various dog clubs. Your dog's expertise will be rewarded with impressive titles. You can participate just for fun, or be competitive and go for those awards.

OBEDIENCE

Training classes begin with pups as young as three months of age in kindergarten puppy training, then advance to pre-novice (all exercises on lead) and go on to novice, which is where you'll start off-lead work. In obedience classes dogs learn to sit, stay, heel and come through a variety of exercises. Once you've got the basics down, you can enter obedience trials and work toward earning your dog's first degree, a C.D. (Companion Dog).

The next level is called "Open," in which jumps and retrieves perk up the dog's interest. Passing grades in competition at this level earn a C.D.X. (Companion Dog Excellent). Beyond that lies the goal of the most ambitious—Utility (U.D. and even U.D.X. or OTCh, an Obedience Champion).

AGILITY

All dogs can participate in the latest canine sport to have gained worldwide popularity for its fun and excitement, agility. It began in England as a canine version of horse show-jumping, but because dogs are more agile and able to perform on verbal commands, extra feats were added such as climbing, balancing and racing through tunnels or in and out of weave poles.

Many of the obstacles (regulation or homemade) can be set up in your own backyard. If the agility bug bites, you could end up in international competition!

For starters, your dog should be obedience trained, even though, in the beginning, the lessons may all be taught on lead. Once the dog understands the commands (and you do, too), it's as easy as guiding the dog over a prescribed course, one obstacle at a time. In competition, the race is against the clock, so wear your running shoes! The dog starts with 200 points and the judge deducts for infractions and misadventures along the way.

All dogs seem to love agility and respond to it as if they were being turned loose in a playground paradise. Your dog's enthusiasm will be contagious; agility turns into great fun for dog and owner.

FIELD TRIALS AND HUNTING TESTS

There are field trials and hunting tests for the sporting breeds—retrievers, spaniels and pointing breeds, and for some hounds—Bassets, Beagles and Dachshunds. Field trials are competitive events that test a dog's ability to perform the functions for which she was bred. Hunting tests, which are open to retrievers,

---

TITLES AWARDED BY THE AKC

Conformation: Ch. (Champion)

Obedience: CD (Companion Dog); CDX (Companion Dog Excellent); UD (Utility Dog); UDX (Utility Dog Excellent); OTCh. (Obedience Trial Champion)

Field: JH (Junior Hunter); SH (Senior Hunter); MH (Master Hunter); AFCh. (Amateur Field Champion); FCh. (Field Champion)

Lure Coursing: JC (Junior Courser); SC (Senior Courser)

Herding: HT (Herding Tested); PT (Pre-Trial Tested); HS (Herding Started); HI (Herding Intermediate); HX (Herding Excellent); HCh. (Herding Champion)

Tracking: TD (Tracking Dog); TDX (Tracking Dog Excellent)

Agility: NAD (Novice Agility); OAD (Open Agility); ADX (Agility Excellent); MAX (Master Agility)

Earthdog Tests: JE (Junior Earthdog); SE (Senior Earthdog); ME (Master Earthdog)

Canine Good Citizen: CGC

Combination: DC (Dual Champion—Ch. and Fch.); TC (Triple Champion—Ch., Fch., and OTCh.)

spaniels and pointing breeds only, are noncompetitive and are a means of judging the dog's ability as well as that of the handler.

Hunting is a very large and complex part of canine sports, and if you own one of the breeds that hunts, the events are a great treat for your dog and you. He gets to do what he was bred for, and you get to work with him and watch him do it. You'll be proud of and amazed at what your dog can do.

Fortunately, the AKC publishes a series of booklets on these events, which outline the rules and regulations and include a glossary of the sometimes complicated terms. The AKC also publishes newsletters for field trialers and hunting test enthusiasts. The United Kennel Club (UKC) also has informative materials for the hunter and his dog.

Retrievers and other sporting breeds get to do what they're bred to in hunting tests.

HERDING TESTS AND TRIALS

Herding, like hunting, dates back to the first known uses man made of dogs. The interest in herding today is widespread, and if you own a herding breed, you can join in the activity. Herding dogs are tested for their natural skills to keep a flock of ducks, sheep or cattle together. If your dog shows potential, you can start at the testing level, where your dog can earn a title for showing an inherent herding ability. With training you can advance to the trial level, where your dog should be capable of controlling even difficult livestock in diverse situations.

LURE COURSING

The AKC Tests and Trials for Lure Coursing are open to traditional sighthounds—Greyhounds, Whippets,

Borzoi, Salukis, Afghan Hounds, Ibizan Hounds and Scottish Deerhounds—as well as to Basenjis and Rhodesian Ridgebacks. Hounds are judged on overall ability, follow, speed, agility and endurance. This is possibly the most exciting of the trials for spectators, because the speed and agility of the dogs is awesome to watch as they chase the lure (or "course") in heats of two or three dogs at a time.

TRACKING

Tracking is another activity in which almost any dog can compete because every dog that sniffs the ground when taken outdoors is, in fact, tracking. The hard part comes when the rules as to what, when and where the dog tracks are determined by a person, not the dog! Tracking tests cover a large area of fields, woods and roads. The tracks are laid hours before the dogs go to work on them, and include "tricks" like cross-tracks and sharp turns. If you're interested in search-and-rescue work, this is the place to start.

This tracking dog is hot on the trail.

EARTHDOG TESTS FOR SMALL TERRIERS AND DACHSHUNDS

These tests are open to Australian, Bedlington, Border, Cairn, Dandie Dinmont, Smooth and Wire Fox, Lakeland, Norfolk, Norwich, Scottish, Sealyham, Skye, Welsh and West Highland White Terriers as well as Dachshunds. The dogs need no prior training for this terrier sport. There is a qualifying test on the day of the event, so dog and handler learn the rules on the spot. These tests, or "digs," sometimes end with informal races in the late afternoon.

133

Here are some of the extracurricular obedience and racing activities that are not regulated by the AKC or UKC, but are generally run by clubs or a group of dog fanciers and are often open to all.

Canine Freestyle This activity is something new on the scene and is variously likened to dancing, dressage or ice skating. It is meant to show the athleticism of the dog, but also requires showmanship on the part of the dog's handler. If you and your dog like to ham it up for friends, you might want to look into freestyle.

Lure coursing lets sighthounds do what they do best—run!

Scent Hurdle Racing Scent hurdle racing is purely a fun activity sponsored by obedience clubs with members forming competing teams. The height of the hurdles is based on the size of the shortest dog on the team. On a signal, one team dog is released on each of two side-by-side courses and must clear every hurdle before picking up its own dumbbell from a platform and returning over the jumps to the handler. As each dog returns, the next on that team is sent. Of course, that is what the dogs are supposed to do. When the dogs improvise (going under or around the hurdles, stealing another dog's dumbbell, and so forth), it no doubt frustrates the handlers, but just adds to the fun for everyone else.

Flyball This type of racing is similar, but after negotiating the four hurdles, the dog comes to a flyball box, steps on a lever that releases a tennis ball into the air, catches the ball and returns over the hurdles to the starting point. This game also becomes extremely fun for spectators because the dogs sometimes cheat by catching a ball released by the dog in the next lane. Three titles can be earned—Flyball Dog (F.D.), Flyball Dog Excellent (F.D.X.) and Flyball Dog Champion (Fb.D.Ch.)—all awarded by the North American Flyball Association, Inc.

Dogsledding The name conjures up the Rocky Mountains or the frigid North, but you can find dogsled clubs in such unlikely spots as Maryland, North Carolina and Virginia! Dogsledding is primarily for the Nordic breeds such as the Alaskan Malamutes, Siberian Huskies and Samoyeds, but other breeds can try. There are some practical backyard applications to this sport, too. With parental supervision, almost any strong dog could pull a child's sled.

Coming over the A-frame on an agility course.

These are just some of the many recreational ways you can get to know and understand your multifaceted dog better and have fun doing it.

10

Your Dog
and your
Family

by Bardi McLennan

Adding a dog automatically increases your family by one, no matter whether you live alone in an apartment or are part of a mother, father and six kids household. The single-person family is fair game for numerous and varied canine misconceptions as to who is dog and who pays the bills, whereas a dog in a houseful of children will consider himself to be just one of the gang, littermates all. One dog and one child may give a dog reason to believe they are both kids or both dogs.

Either interpretation requires parental supervision and sometimes speedy intervention.

As soon as one paw goes through the door into your home, Rufus (or Rufina) has to make many adjustments to become a part of your family. Your job is to make him fit in as painlessly as possible. An older dog may have some frame of reference from past experience, but to a 10-week-old puppy, everything is brand new: people, furniture, stairs, when and where people eat, sleep or watch TV, his own place and everyone else's space, smells, sounds, outdoors—everything!

Puppies, and newly acquired dogs of any age, do not need what we think of as "freedom." If you leave a new dog or puppy loose in the house, you will almost certainly return to chaotic destruction and the dog will forever after equate your homecoming with a time of punishment to be dreaded. It is unfair to give your dog what amounts to "freedom to get into trouble." Instead, confine him to a crate for brief periods of your absence (up to three or four hours) and, for the long haul, a workday for example, confine him to one untrashable area with his own toys, a bowl of water and a radio left on (low) in another room.

Lots of pets get along with each other just fine.

For the first few days, when not confined, put Rufus on a long leash tied to your wrist or waist. This umbilical cord method enables the dog to learn all about you from your body language and voice, and to learn by his own actions which things in the house are NO! and which ones are rewarded by "Good dog." House-training will be easier with the pup always by your side. Speaking of which, accidents do happen. That goal of "completely housetrained" takes up to a year, or the length of time it takes the pup to mature.

The All-Adult Family

Most dogs in an adults-only household today are likely to be latchkey pets, with no one home all day but the dog. When you return after a tough day on the job, the dog can and should be your relaxation therapy. But going home can instead be a daily frustration.

Separation anxiety is a very common problem for the dog in a working household. It may begin with whines and barks of loneliness, but it will soon escalate into a frenzied destruction derby. That is why it is so important to set aside the time to teach a dog to relax when left alone in his confined area and to understand that he can trust you to return.

Let the dog get used to your work schedule in easy stages. Confine him to one room and go in and out of that room over and over again. Be casual about it. No physical, voice or eye contact. When the pup no longer even notices your comings and goings, leave the house for varying lengths of time, returning to stay home for a few minutes and gradually increasing the time away. This training can take days, but the dog is learning that you haven't left him forever and that he can trust you.

Any time you leave the dog, but especially during this training period, be casual about your departure. No anxiety-building fond farewells. Just "Bye" and go! Remember the "Good dog" when you return to find everything more or less as you left it.

If things are a mess (or even a disaster) when you return, greet the dog, take him outside to eliminate, and then put him in his crate while you clean up. Rant and rave in the shower! *Do not* punish the dog. You were not there when it happened, and the rule is: Only punish as you catch the dog in the act of wrongdoing. Obviously, it makes sense to get your latchkey puppy when you'll have a week or two to spend on these training essentials.

Family weekend activities should include Rufus whenever possible. Depending on the pup's age, now is the time for a long walk in the park, playtime in the backyard, a hike in the woods. Socializing is as important as health care, good food and physical exercise, so visiting Aunt Emma or Uncle Harry and the next-door neighbor's dog or cat is essential to developing an outgoing, friendly temperament in your pet.

If you are a single adult, socializing Rufus at home and away will prevent him from becoming overly protective of you (or just overly attached) and will also prevent such behavioral problems as dominance or fear of strangers.

Babies

Whether already here or on the way, babies figure larger than life in the eyes of a dog. If the dog is there first, let him in on all your baby preparations in the house. When baby arrives, let Rufus sniff any item of clothing that has been on the baby before Junior comes home. Then let Mom greet the dog first before introducing the new family member. Hold the baby down for the dog to see and sniff, but make sure someone's holding the dog on lead in case of any sudden moves. Don't play keep-away or tease the dog with the baby, which only invites undesirable jumping up.

The dog and the baby are "family," and for starters can be treated almost as equals. Things rapidly change, however, especially when baby takes to creeping around on all fours on the dog's turf or, better yet, has yummy pudding all over her face and hands! That's when a lot of things in the dog's and baby's lives become more separate than equal.

Dogs are perfect confidants.

Toddlers make terrible dog owners, but if you can't avoid the combination, use patient discipline (that is, positive teaching rather than punishment), and use time-outs before you run out of patience.

139

A dog and a baby (or toddler, or an assertive young child) should never be left alone together. Take the dog with you or confine him. With a baby or youngsters in the house, you'll have plenty of use for that wonderful canine safety device called a crate!

Young Children

Any dog in a house with kids will behave pretty much as the kids do, good or bad. But even good dogs and good children can get into trouble when play becomes rowdy and active.

Legs bobbing up and down, shrill voices screeching, a ball hurtling overhead, all add up to exuberant frustration for a dog who's just trying to be part of the gang. In a pack of puppies, any legs or toys being chased would be caught by a set of teeth, and all the pups involved would understand that is how the game is played. Kids do not understand this, nor do parents tolerate it. Bring Rufus indoors before you have reason to regret it. This is time-out, not a punishment.

Teach children how to play nicely with a puppy.

You can explain the situation to the children and tell them they must play quieter games until the puppy learns not to grab them with his mouth. Unfortunately, you can't explain it that easily to the dog. With adult supervision, they will learn how to play together.

Young children love to tease. Sticking their faces or wiggling their hands or fingers in the dog's face is teasing. To another person it might be just annoying, but it is threatening to a dog. There's another difference: We can make the child stop by an explanation, but the only way a dog can stop it is with a warning growl and then with teeth. Teasing is the major cause of children being bitten by their pets. Treat it seriously.

Older Children

The best age for a child to get a first dog is between the ages of 8 and 12. That's when kids are able to accept some real responsibility for their pet. Even so, take the child's vow of "I will never *ever* forget to feed (brush, walk, etc.) the dog" for what it's worth: a child's good intention at that moment. Most kids today have extra lessons, soccer practice, Little League, ballet, and so forth piled on top of school schedules. There will be many times when Mom will have to come to the dog's rescue. "I walked the dog for you so you can set the table for me" is one way to get around a missed appointment without laying on blame or guilt.

Kids in this age group make excellent obedience trainers because they are into the teaching/learning process themselves and they lack the self-consciousness of adults. Attending a dog show is something the whole family can enjoy, and watching Junior Showmanship may catch the eye of the kids. Older children can begin to get involved in many of the recreational activities that were reviewed in the previous chapter. Some of the agility obstacles, for example, can be set up in the backyard as a family project (with an adult making sure all the equipment is safe and secure for the dog).

Older kids are also beginning to look to the future, and may envision themselves as veterinarians or trainers or show dog handlers or writers of the next Lassie best-seller. Dogs are perfect confidants for these dreams. They won't tell a soul.

Other Pets

Introduce all pets tactfully. In a dog/cat situation, hold the dog, not the cat. Let two dogs meet on neutral turf—a stroll in the park or a walk down the street—with both on loose leads to permit all the normal canine ways of saying hello, including routine sniffing, circling, more sniffing, and so on. Small creatures such as hamsters, chinchillas or mice must be kept safe from their natural predators (dogs and cats).

Festive Family Occasions

Parties are great for people, but not necessarily for puppies. Until all the guests have arrived, put the dog in his crate or in a room where he won't be disturbed. A socialized dog can join the fun later as long as he's not underfoot, annoying guests or into the hors d'oeuvres.

There are a few dangers to consider, too. Doors opening and closing can allow a puppy to slip out unnoticed in the confusion, and you'll be organizing a search party instead of playing host or hostess. Party food and buffet service are not for dogs. Let Rufus party in his crate with a nice big dog biscuit.

At Christmas time, not only are tree decorations dangerous and breakable (and perhaps family heirlooms), but extreme caution should be taken with the lights, cords and outlets for the tree lights and any other festive lighting. Occasionally a dog lifts a leg, ignoring the fact that the tree is indoors. To avoid this, use a canine repellent, made for gardens, on the tree. Or keep him out of the tree room unless supervised. And whatever you do, *don't* invite trouble by hanging his toys on the tree!

Car Travel

Before you plan a vacation by car or RV with Rufus, be sure he enjoys car travel. Nothing spoils a holiday quicker than a carsick dog! Work within the dog's comfort level. Get in the car with the dog in his crate or attached to a canine car safety belt and just sit there until he relaxes. That's all. Next time, get in the car, turn on the engine and go nowhere. Just sit. When that is okay, turn on the engine and go around the block. Now you can go for a ride and include a stop where you get out, leaving the dog for a minute or two.

On a warm day, always park in the shade and leave windows open several inches. And return quickly. It only takes 10 minutes for a car to become an overheated steel death trap.

Motel or Pet Motel?

Not all motels or hotels accept pets, but you have a much better choice today than even a few years ago. To find a dog-friendly lodging, look at *On the Road Again With Man's Best Friend*, a series of directories that detail bed and breakfasts, inns, family resorts and other hotels/motels. Some places require a refundable deposit to cover any damage incurred by the dog. More B&Bs accept pets now, but some restrict the size.

If taking Rufus with you is not feasible, check out boarding kennels in your area. Your veterinarian may offer this service, or recommend a kennel or two he or she is familiar with. Go see the facilities for yourself, ask about exercise, diet, housing, and so on. Or, if you'd rather have Rufus stay home, look into bonded petsitters, many of whom will also bring in the mail and water your plants.

chapter 11

Your Dog
and your
Community

by Bardi McLennan

Step outside your home with your dog and you are no longer just family, you are both part of your community. This is when the phrase "responsible pet ownership" takes on serious implications. For starters, it means you pick up after your dog—not just occasionally, but every time your dog eliminates away from home. That means you have joined the Plastic Baggy Brigade! You always have plastic sandwich bags in your pocket and several in the car. It means you teach your kids how to use them, too. If you think this is "yucky," just imagine what the person (a non-doggy person) who inadvertently steps in the mess thinks!

Your responsibility extends to your neighbors: To their ears (no annoying barking); to their property (their garbage, their lawn, their flower beds, their cat—especially their cat); to their kids (on bikes, at play); to their kids' toys and sports equipment.

There are numerous dog-related laws, ranging from simple dog licensing and leash laws to those holding you liable for any physical injury or property damage done by your dog. These laws are in place to protect everyone in the community, including you and your dog. There are town ordinances and state laws which are by no means the same in all towns or all states. Ignorance of the law won't get you off the hook. The time to find out what the laws are where you live is now.

Be sure your dog's license is current. This is not just a good local ordinance, it can make the difference between finding your lost dog or not. Many states now require proof of rabies vaccination and that the dog has been spayed or neutered before issuing a license. At the same time, keep up the dog's annual immunizations.

Dressing your dog up makes him appealing to strangers.

Never let your dog run loose in the neighborhood. This will not only keep you on the right side of the leash law, it's the outdoor version of the rule about not giving your dog "freedom to get into trouble."

Good Canine Citizen

Sometimes it's hard for a dog's owner to assess whether or not the dog is sufficiently socialized to be accepted by the community at large. Does Rufus or Rufina display good, controlled behavior in public? The AKC's Canine Good Citizen program is available through many dog organizations. If your dog passes the test, the title "CGC" is earned.

The overall purpose is to turn your dog into a good neighbor and to teach you about your responsibility to your community as a dog owner. Here are the ten things your dog must do willingly:

1. Accept a stranger stopping to chat with you.
2. Sit and be petted by a stranger.
3. Allow a stranger to handle him or her as a groomer or veterinarian would.
4. Walk nicely on a loose lead.
5. Walk calmly through a crowd.
6. Sit and down on command, then stay in a sit or down position while you walk away.
7. Come when called.
8. Casually greet another dog.
9. React confidently to distractions.
10. Accept being left alone with someone other than you and not become overly agitated or nervous.

Schools and Dogs

Schools are getting involved with pet ownership on an educational level. It has been proven that children who are kind to animals are humane in their attitude toward other people as adults.

A dog is a child's best friend, and so children are often primary pet owners, if not the primary caregivers. Unfortunately, they are also the ones most often bitten by dogs. This occurs due to a lack of understanding that pets, no matter how sweet, cuddly and loving, are still animals. Schools, along with parents, dog clubs, dog fanciers and the AKC, are working to change all that with video programs for children not only in grade school, but in the nursery school and pre-kindergarten age group. Teaching youngsters how to be responsible dog owners is important community work. When your dog has a CGC, volunteer to take part in an educational classroom event put on by your dog club.

Boy Scout Merit Badge

A Merit Badge for Dog Care can be earned by any Boy Scout ages 11 to 18. The requirements are not easy, but amount to a complete course in responsible dog care and general ownership. Here are just a few of the things a Scout must do to earn that badge:

> Point out ten parts of the dog using the correct names.

> Give a report (signed by parent or guardian) on your care of the dog (feeding, food used, housing, exercising, grooming and bathing), plus what has been done to keep the dog healthy.

> Explain the right way to obedience train a dog, and demonstrate three comments.

> Several of the requirements have to do with health care, including first aid, handling a hurt dog, and the dangers of home treatment for a serious ailment.

> The final requirement is to know the local laws and ordinances involving dogs.

There are similar programs for Girl Scouts and 4-H members.

Local Clubs

Local dog clubs are no longer in existence just to put on a yearly dog show. Today, they are apt to be the hub of the community's involvement with pets. Dog clubs conduct educational forums with big-name speakers, stage demonstrations of canine talent in a busy mall and take dogs of various breeds to schools for classroom discussion.

The quickest way to feel accepted as a member in a club is to volunteer your services! Offer to help with something—anything—and watch your popularity (and your interest) grow.

Therapy Dogs

Once your dog has earned that essential CGC and reliably demonstrates a steady, calm temperament, you could look into what therapy dogs are doing in your area.

Therapy dogs go with their owners to visit patients at hospitals or nursing homes, generally remaining on leash but able to coax a pat from a stiffened hand, a smile from a blank face, a few words from sealed lips or a hug from someone in need of love.

Nursing homes cover a wide range of patient care. Some specialize in care of the elderly, some in the treatment of specific illnesses, some in physical therapy. Children's facilities also welcome visits from trained therapy dogs for boosting morale in their pediatric patients. Hospice care for the terminally ill and the at-home care of AIDS patients are other areas where this canine visiting is desperately needed. Therapy dog training comes first.

Your dog can make a difference in lots of lives.

There is a lot more involved than just taking your nice friendly pooch to someone's bedside. Doing therapy dog work involves your own emotional stability as well as that of your dog. But once you have met all the requirements for this work, making the rounds once a week or once a month with your therapy dog is possibly the most rewarding of all community activities.

Disaster Aid

This community service is definitely not for everyone, partly because it is time-consuming. The initial training is rigorous, and there can be no let-up in the continuing workouts, because members are on call 24 hours a day to go wherever they are needed at a

148

moment's notice. But if you think you would like to be able to assist in a disaster, look into search-and-rescue work. The network of search-and-rescue volunteers is worldwide, and all members of the American Rescue Dog Association (ARDA) who are qualified to do this work are volunteers who train and maintain their own dogs.

Physical Aid

Most people are familiar with Seeing Eye dogs, which serve as blind people's eyes, but not with all the other work that dogs are trained to do to assist the disabled. Dogs are also specially trained to pull wheelchairs, carry school books, pick up dropped objects, open and close doors. Some also are ears for the deaf. All these assistance-trained dogs, by the way, are allowed anywhere "No Pet" signs exist (as are therapy dogs when

Making the rounds with your therapy dog can be very rewarding.

properly identified). Getting started in any of this fascinating work requires a background in dog training and canine behavior, but there are also volunteer jobs ranging from answering the phone to cleaning out kennels to providing a foster home for a puppy. You have only to ask.

part four

Beyond
the
Basics

chapter 12

Recommended Reading

Books

ABOUT HEALTH CARE

Ackerman, Lowell. *Guide to Skin and Haircoat Problems in Dogs.* Loveland, Colo.: Alpine Publications, 1994.

Alderton, David. *The Dog Care Manual.* Hauppauge, N.Y.: Barron's Educational Series, Inc., 1986.

American Kennel Club. *American Kennel Club Dog Care and Training.* New York· Howell Book House, 1991.

Bamberger, Michelle, DVM. *Help! The Quick Guide to First Aid for Your Dog.* New York: Howell Book House, 1995.

Carlson, Delbert, DVM, and James Giffin, MD. *Dog Owner's Home Veterinary Handbook.* New York: Howell Book House, 1992.

DeBitetto, James, DVM, and Sarah Hodgson. *You & Your Puppy.* New York: Howell Book House, 1995.

Humphries, Jim, DVM. *Dr. Jim's Animal Clinic for Dogs.* New York: Howell Book House, 1994.

McGinnis, Terri. *The Well Dog Book.* New York: Random House, 1991.

Pitcairn, Richard and Susan. *Natural Health for Dogs.* Emmaus, Pa.: Rodale Press, 1982.

ABOUT DOG SHOWS

Hall, Lynn. *Dog Showing for Beginners.* New York: Howell Book House, 1994.

Nichols, Virginia Tuck. *How to Show Your Own Dog.* Neptune, N. J.: TFH, 1970.

Vanacore, Connie. *Dog Showing, An Owner's Guide.* New York: Howell Book House, 1990.

ABOUT TRAINING

Ammen, Amy. *Training in No Time*. New York: Howell Book House, 1995.

Baer, Ted. *Communicating With Your Dog*. Hauppauge, N.Y.: Barron's Educational Series, Inc., 1989.

Benjamin, Carol Lea. *Dog Problems*. New York: Howell Book House, 1989.

Benjamin, Carol Lea. *Dog Training for Kids*. New York: Howell Book House, 1988.

Benjamin, Carol Lea. *Mother Knows Best*. New York: Howell Book House, 1985.

Benjamin, Carol Lea. *Surviving Your Dog's Adolescence*. New York: Howell Book House, 1993.

Bohnenkamp, Gwen. *Manners for the Modern Dog*. San Francisco: Perfect Paws, 1990.

Dibra, Bashkim. *Dog Training by Bash*. New York: Dell, 1992.

Dunbar, Ian, PhD, MRCVS. *Dr. Dunbar's Good Little Dog Book*, James & Kenneth Publishers, 2140 Shattuck Ave. #2406, Berkeley, Calif. 94704. (510) 658–8588. Order from the publisher.

Dunbar, Ian, PhD, MRCVS. *How to Teach a New Dog Old Tricks*, James & Kenneth Publishers. Order from the publisher; address above.

Dunbar, Ian, PhD, MRCVS, and Gwen Bohnenkamp. Booklets on *Preventing Aggression; Housetraining; Chewing; Digging; Barking; Socialization; Fearfulness; and Fighting*, James & Kenneth Publishers. Order from the publisher; address above.

Evans, Job Michael. *People, Pooches and Problems*. New York: Howell Book House, 1991.

Kilcommons, Brian and Sarah Wilson. *Good Owners, Great Dogs*. New York: Warner Books, 1992.

McMains, Joel M. *Dog Logic—Companion Obedience*. New York: Howell Book House, 1992.

Rutherford, Clarice and David H. Neil, MRCVS. *How to Raise a Puppy You Can Live With*. Loveland, Colo.: Alpine Publications, 1982.

Volhard, Jack and Melissa Bartlett. *What All Good Dogs Should Know: The Sensible Way to Train*. New York: Howell Book House, 1991.

ABOUT BREEDING

Harris, Beth J. Finder. *Breeding a Litter, The Complete Book of Prenatal and Postnatal Care*. New York: Howell Book House, 1983.

Holst, Phyllis, DVM. *Canine Reproduction*. Loveland, Colo.: Alpine Publications, 1985.

Walkowicz, Chris and Bonnie Wilcox, DVM. *Successful Dog Breeding, The Complete Handbook of Canine Midwifery.* New York: Howell Book House, 1994.

ABOUT ACTIVITIES

American Rescue Dog Association. *Search and Rescue Dogs.* New York: Howell Book House, 1991.

Barwig, Susan and Stewart Hilliard. *Schutzhund.* New York: Howell Book House, 1991.

Beaman, Arthur S. *Lure Coursing.* New York: Howell Book House, 1994.

Daniels, Julie. *Enjoying Dog Agility—From Backyard to Competition.* New York: Doral Publishing, 1990.

Davis, Kathy Diamond. *Therapy Dogs.* New York: Howell Book House, 1992.

Gallup, Davis Anne. *Running With Man's Best Friend.* Loveland, Colo.: Alpine Publications, 1986.

Habgood, Dawn and Robert. *On the Road Again With Man's Best Friend.* New England, Mid-Atlantic, West Coast and Southeast editions. Selective guides to area bed and breakfasts, inns, hotels and resorts that welcome guests and their dogs. New York: Howell Book House, 1995.

Holland, Vergil S. *Herding Dogs.* New York: Howell Book House, 1994.

LaBelle, Charlene G. *Backpacking With Your Dog.* Loveland, Colo.: Alpine Publications, 1993.

Simmons-Moake, Jane. *Agility Training, The Fun Sport for All Dogs.* New York: Howell Book House, 1991.

Spencer, James B. *Hup! Training Flushing Spaniels the American Way.* New York: Howell Book House, 1992.

Spencer, James B. *Point! Training the All-Seasons Birddog.* New York: Howell Book House, 1995.

Tarrant, Bill. *Training the Hunting Retriever.* New York: Howell Book House, 1991.

Volhard, Jack and Wendy. *The Canine Good Citizen.* New York: Howell Book House, 1994.

General Titles

Haggerty, Captain Arthur J. *How to Get Your Pet Into Show Business.* New York: Howell Book House, 1994.

McLennan, Bardi. *Dogs and Kids, Parenting Tips.* New York: Howell Book House, 1993.

Moran, Patti J. *Pet Sitting for Profit, A Complete Manual for Professional Success.* New York: Howell Book House, 1992.

Scalisi, Danny and Libby Moses. *When Rover Just Won't Do, Over 2,000 Suggestions for Naming Your Dog.* New York: Howell Book House, 1993.

Sife, Wallace, PhD. *The Loss of a Pet.* New York: Howell Book House, 1993.

Wrede, Barbara J. *Civilizing Your Puppy.* Hauppauge, N.Y.: Barron's Educational Series, 1992.

Magazines

The AKC GAZETTE, The Official Journal for the Sport of Purebred Dogs. American Kennel Club, 51 Madison Ave., New York, NY.

Bloodlines Journal. United Kennel Club, 100 E. Kilgore Rd., Kalamazoo, MI.

Dog Fancy. Fancy Publications, 3 Burroughs, Irvine, CA 92718

Dog World. Maclean Hunter Publishing Corp., 29 N. Wacker Dr., Chicago, IL 60606.

Videos

"SIRIUS Puppy Training," by Ian Dunbar, PhD, MRCVS. James & Kenneth Publishers, 2140 Shattuck Ave. #2406, Berkeley, CA 94704. Order from the publisher.

"Training the Companion Dog," from Dr. Dunbar's British TV Series, James & Kenneth Publishers. (See address above).

The American Kennel Club produces videos on every breed of dog, as well as on hunting tests, field trials and other areas of interest to purebred dog owners. For more information, write to AKC/Video Fulfillment, 5580 Centerview Dr., Suite 200, Raleigh, NC 27606.

chapter 13

Resources

Breed Clubs

Every breed recognized by the American Kennel Club has a national (parent) club. National clubs are a great source of information on your breed. You can get the name of the secretary of the club by contacting:

The American Kennel Club
51 Madison Avenue
New York, NY 10010
(212) 696-8200

There are also numerous all-breed, individual breed, obedience, hunting and other special-interest dog clubs across the country. The American Kennel Club can provide you with a geographical list of clubs to find ones in your area. Contact them at the above address.

Registry Organizations

Registry organizations register purebred dogs. The American Kennel Club is the oldest and largest in this country, and currently recognizes over 130 breeds. The United Kennel Club registers some breeds the AKC doesn't (including the American Pit Bull Terrier and the Miniature Fox Terrier) as well as many of the same breeds. The others included here are for your reference; the AKC can provide you with a list of foreign registries.

American Kennel Club
51 Madison Avenue
New York, NY 10010

United Kennel Club (UKC)
100 E. Kilgore Road
Kalamazoo, MI 49001-5598

American Dog Breeders Assn.
P.O. Box 1771
Salt Lake City, UT 84110
(Registers American Pit Bull Terriers)

Canadian Kennel Club
89 Skyway Avenue
Etobicoke, Ontario
Canada M9W 6R4

National Stock Dog Registry
P.O. Box 402
Butler, IN 46721
(Registers working stock dogs)

Orthopedic Foundation for Animals (OFA)
2300 E. Nifong Blvd.
Columbia, MO 65201-3856
(Hip registry)

Activity Clubs

Write to these organizations for information on the activities they sponsor.

American Kennel Club
51 Madison Avenue
New York, NY 10010
(Conformation Shows, Obedience Trials, Field Trials and Hunting Tests, Agility, Canine Good

Citizen, Lure Coursing, Herding, Tracking, Earthdog Tests, Coonhunting.)

United Kennel Club
100 E. Kilgore Road
Kalamazoo, MI 49001-5598
(Conformation Shows, Obedience Trials, Agility, Hunting for Various Breeds, Terrier Trials and more.)

North American Flyball Assn.
1342 Jeff St.
Ypsilanti, MI 48198

International Sled Dog Racing Assn.
P.O. Box 446
Norman, ID 83848-0446

North American Working Dog Assn., Inc.
Southeast Kreisgruppe
P.O. Box 833
Brunswick, GA 31521

Trainers

Association of Pet Dog Trainers
P.O. Box 3734
Salinas, CA 93912
(408) 663–9257

American Dog Trainers' Network
161 West 4th St.
New York, NY 10014
(212) 727–7257

National Association of Dog Obedience Instructors
2286 East Steel Rd.
St. Johns, MI 48879

Associations

American Dog Owners Assn.
1654 Columbia Tpke.
Castleton, NY 12033
(Works on anti-dog legislation)

Delta Society
P.O. Box 1080
Renton, WA 98057-9906
(Promotes the human/animal bond through
pet-assisted therapy and other programs)

Dog Writers Assn. of America (DWAA)
Sally Cooper, Secy.
222 Woodchuck Ln.
Harwinton, CT 06791

National Assn. for Search and Rescue (NASAR)
P.O. Box 3709
Fairfax, VA 22038

Therapy Dogs International
6 Hilltop Road
Mendham, NJ 07945